101 Questions & Answers about STANDARDS, ASSESSMENT, and ACCOUNTABILITY

Other Books by This Author

Accountability for Learning:
How Teachers and School Leaders Can Take Charge

Accountability in Action:
A Blueprint for Learning Organizations, 2nd Ed.

Assessing Educational Leaders:
Evaluating Performance for Improved Individual and Organizational Results

Daily Disciplines of Leadership:
How to Improve Student Achievement, Staff Motivation, and Personal Organization

Holistic Accountability:
Serving Students, Schools, and Community

The Leader's Guide to Standards:
A Blueprint for Educational Equity and Excellence

The Learning Leader: How to Focus School Improvement for Better Results

Making Standards Work:
Implementing Standards-Based Assessments in the Classroom, School, and District, 3rd Ed.

On Common Ground:
The Power of Professional Learning Communities

101 More Questions and Answers about Standards, Assessment, and Accountability

Reason to Write:
Help Your Child Succeed in School and in Life Through Better Reasoning and Clear Communication

Reason to Write Student Handbook

Reframing Teacher Leadership to Improve Your School

For a listing of current articles in periodicals, please visit www.LeadandLearn.com

101 Questions & Answers about STANDARDS, ASSESSMENT, and ACCOUNTABILITY

LEAD+
LEARN
PRESS

Douglas B. Reeves, Ph.D.

LEAD+
LEARN
PRESS

Lead + Learn Press
317 Inverness Way South, Suite 150
Englewood, Colorado 80112
Phone +1.866.399.6019 • Fax 303.504.9417
www.LeadandLearn.com

All Web links in this book are correct as of the publication date below but may have become inactive or otherwise modified since that time. If you notice a deactivated or changed link, please notify the publisher and specify the Web link, the book title, and the page number on which the link appears so that corrections may be made in future editions.

Lead + Learn Press also publishes books in a variety of electronic formats. Some content that appears in print may not be available in electronic books.

Editor: Allison Wedell Schumacher

Library of Congress Cataloging-in-Publication Data:

Reeves, Douglas B., 1953–

101 questions and answers about standards, assessment, and accountability / by Douglas B. Reeves.

p. cm.

Includes bibliographical references (p.) and index.

ISBN 978-0-9644955-7-9

1. Education--Standards--United States--Miscellanea. 2. Education--United States--Evaluation--Miscellanea. 3. Educational accountability--United States--Miscellanea. I. Title: 101 questions and answers about standards, assessment, and accountability. II. Title: One hundred one questions & answers about standards, assessment, and accountability. III. Title: One hundred and one questions & answers about standards, assessment, and accountability. IV. Title.

LB3060.83 .R44 2000
379.1'58'0973--dc21 00-052562

Printed and bound in the United States of America

12 11 10 09 08 08 09 10

About the Author

Dr. Douglas Reeves is founder of The Leadership and Learning Center, an international organization dedicated to improving student achievement and educational equity. Through its long-term relationships with school systems, The Center helps educators and school leaders improve student achievement through practical and constructive approaches to standards, assessment, and accountability.

Dr. Reeves is a frequent keynote speaker in the U.S. and abroad for education, government, and business organizations and is a faculty member of leadership programs sponsored by the Harvard Graduate School of Education. The author of twenty books and many articles, Doug is the author of the best-selling *Making Standards Work*, now in its third edition. In addition to his numerous publications, Dr. Reeves' work can be seen in national journals, magazines, and newspapers. Doug has twice been selected for the Harvard Distinguished Authors Series and he recently won the Parents' Choice Award for his writing for children and parents.

Beyond his work in large-scale assessment and research, Doug has devoted many years to classroom teaching with students ranging from elementary school to doctoral candidates. Doug's family includes four children ranging from elementary school through college, all of whom have attended public schools. His wife, Shelley Sackett, is an attorney, mediator, and school board member. He lives near Boston and can be reached at dreeves@LeadandLearn.com.

Contents

Introduction

The standards movement is at a crossroads. Behind us lie some extraordinary areas of progress and more than a few mistakes. Well-intentioned people continue to debate the standards movement vigorously, and many of those issues have been raised by the thousands of people who have taken time to write, call, or e-mail the questions which have been distilled in this volume. Many things have changed in the standards movement in the past decade, but the fundamentals have not. First, when standards are properly implemented, students, parents, and teachers know the "rules of the game" and thus have clear expectations that do not vary with neighborhood, economic status, or skin color. Second, the appropriate use of standards creates a framework, not a straitjacket. Within that framework, there remains enormous room for creativity and freedom. With standards, individual student variation is recognized and cherished. Variations among students lead to changes in strategy, not to diminished expectations. Creativity and freedom do not extend to the choice of denying students high expectations and academic success based on idiosyncratic judgments of individual teachers or administrators. Third and most importantly, the alternative to academic standards is not educational paradise, but a retreat to the 1950s in which the designation of students as bluebirds, robins, and blackbirds was no more accidental than the colors associated with those labels.

Despite the compelling and fundamental truths that standards are fair and effective, there is a growing movement to abandon standards and the frequent allegation that standards are a danger to student success. There are, in fact, persuasive arguments against bad standards. Indeed, some state and local standards are poorly worded and ineptly implemented. It does not logically follow that an attack on poor standards constitutes a persuasive argument against all standards, and certainly not against standards implemented judiciously and with care. The occasional misuse of a syringe does not justify the abandonment of smallpox vaccinations. We have a consensus that school children should be vaccinated not because we have universal agreement on all health issues, but because there are some central truths of disease prevention and values of mutual interest that govern this policy. Let me suggest that the academic and emotional health of our students must be taken as seriously as their physical health. If we would not send a child to school without appropriate vaccinations, then we dare not send them into the world without the knowledge and skills to succeed. We nurture the emotional health of students not by coddling them and lowering our expectations, but by giving them the tools and the time necessary to succeed.

What follows in these pages is a dialog between sincere questioners and a fellow learner. It is perhaps presumptuous to suggest that my responses are "answers" because as a teacher I am, above all, a learner acutely aware of my limitations and the inadequacy of simple answers to complex challenges. The responses in the following pages should thus be viewed as an invitation to continued exploration and discussion and not the final word on any matter. At the very least, the responses offer practical advice based on observations of teachers, students, and school leaders in thousands of schools on four continents. These people have been my most valuable tutors and my debt is inadequately paid by the thanks expressed here. I can only hope that the hours devoted to being the volunteer "test doctor" of the Internet (an unpaid job that entails responding to 80–90 e-mails a day from students, teachers, parents, and school leaders) are partial payment for the wonderful lessons I have received.

My defense of standards is not a protection of the many deeply flawed standards and the egregious examples of mindless test preparation masquerading as rigorous academic standards. In the end, reforming standards and educating practitioners and leaders will advance the cause of reason far more than the abandonment of a movement that offers equity, excellence, and coherence in public education.

Writers, like teachers, are creatures of collaboration. My collaborators have included an insightful and challenging editor, Allison Wedell Schumacher, and my other colleagues at The Leadership and Learning Center. I am grateful to Amy Whited, our former "testdoctor hotline" monitor, for giving me a springboard of frequently asked questions from which to work. I am also indebted to Larry Ainsworth, Eileen Allison, Chris Benavides, Audrey Blackwell, Kathi Lambert, Michele Lopez, Matthew Mason, Terry Osner, Devon

Sheldon, Glenda Sinks, and Mike White, all of whom have devoted their careers to listening to, supporting, and working with educators and school leaders. The students in our household, Brooks, Alex, Julia, and James, bear the misfortune of having every assignment scrutinized and potentially used as an example in a workshop or seminar. They have been among my best teachers, even when both teacher and student were reluctant participants in the collaboration. The refrain they have heard so often is the appropriate one with which to begin this dialog: "I didn't say it would be easy; I just said it was necessary."

Douglas Reeves
Denver, Colorado
November 2000

CHAPTER 1

Standards

Standards: What They Are and Why We Need Them

1 What is this 'standards movement' I keep hearing about, and how will it affect my child?

The "standards movement" is hardly a new and revolutionary idea. In every school in the country, there are athletic teams and musical groups that routinely take a "standards-based" approach to education. When students fail to make a free throw in basketball or hit an F-sharp in band, they do not receive a "B-" in those subjects. Rather, those students get immediate feedback that they did not "meet the standard" and then use that feedback to improve their performance. Essentially, the standards movement asks parents, teachers, and students to apply the same techniques to academic classes.

The most important reason for you to support academic standards in your school is that the standards are a fair and effective way to give students the "rules of the game" when they are in school. By comparing one child's performance to a clear standard, parents, children, and teachers all know precisely what is expected. Every time the child attempts a task, the performance is compared to the standard, not to other children's performances. The most important advantages for children and parents are fairness, clarity, and improved learning. Standards are fair because the student knows what must be done before the task is attempted. In schools without clear standards, the performance of one student is usually compared to that of another child. In these circumstances, we never know if we have succeeded until *after* the performance is compared to that of other students. In a standards-based system, the rules are clear: Either the student meets the standard or the student does not. If the standard is not met, the student typically receives another opportunity to become proficient.

Many excellent teachers have long used the standards-based approach in their classes. Their students know what is expected of them, and the definition of success is never a mystery. In the classes taught by these outstanding teachers, student achievement soars because everyone knows that success is defined by the achievement of a standard, and not merely by beating other students or guessing what the teacher wants. In other classrooms, unfortunately, standards are utterly absent. In these classes, the expectations of students are a mystery. I've heard teachers say, "I give the best papers an A and the rest are Bs." In other cases, teachers say, "I can't really describe what acceptable student work is, but I know it when I see it." In both of these cases, students are doomed to an ineffectual guessing game. With clear standards, teachers, students, and parents know what is expected, and success is the result of hard work, not speculation or luck.

Q

2 Standards terminology is confusing. I've heard the words "standard" or "benchmark" or "performance standard" or "curriculum objective" all used to refer to the *same* thing. It's maddening. Can you make sense out of this?

A Unfortunately, different states have used different terminology, and there is little consistency in the standards literature about the use of these terms. Nevertheless, let me give it a try. Whatever terms your state uses, we progress from the most general descriptions of what students should know and do to the most specific descriptions. For example, if this were a discussion of student discipline, we might have a general standard that "students will be well-behaved in class" and a specific expectation that "students will participate in discussions actively and respectfully, supporting their ideas with facts and avoiding interruption of others." In the academic context, a general expectation might be that the student will "apply mathematics to real world problem-solving" and a specific expectation might be that the student will "accurately describe, using words, mathematical symbols, and graphs, the growth of money over ten years at a given rate of interest." Of course, these specific expectations would vary depending on the grade-level of the students.

The term most frequently applied to general expectations of student knowledge is "academic content standards." Many different terms have been used to refer to specific expectations that students must meet at certain grade levels. Some states, for example, use the term "benchmarks" to describe the knowledge and skills that students must have as they pass certain thresholds (typically grades 4, 8, and 12). Other states use terms such as "performance standards" or "curriculum objectives" to describe the specific learning objectives associated with different grade levels.

The final and most important level of specificity in standards-based education is the "scoring guide" or "rubric." This provides the very specific expectations of what students must do in order to provide evidence that they have achieved a standard or benchmark. Although there is much public debate about the academic content standards and much confusion about benchmarks and other terms for grade-level expectations, the most important element of standards is the scoring guide. This tells the student and parent in clear and specific terms what academic success looks like. You simply cannot have effective implementation of standards without clear, comprehensive, and consistent scoring guides.

Q 3 **I'm concerned that the standards movement may simply be a top-down mechanism of uniformity and convergent thinking. How can you prove that standards will result in student achievement? Don't the actual practices of teachers have something to do with it? Or perhaps the only relevant standard for any individual student is the proximal zone of development.**

A Your question contains an essential truth: The mere establishment of standards is useless without the hard work of teachers, school leaders, parents, and students. Only "actual practices of teachers" result in achievement. As I have frequently said to audiences of teachers and school leaders, merely decorating rooms with colorful posters of standards from the state department of education is a futile exercise. The impact of standards can only occur when teachers collaborate and reach a consensus on the meaning of standards and proficiency.

Standards are, indeed, important. They are the heart of fairness in the classroom, and many effective teachers have long had clear standards of performance for students. But standards are not a magical potion from state departments, professional organizations, or consultants. They are a device for assessing student performance compared to an immutable objective rather than comparing one student to another. No standard or assessment has value without insightful, professional, and caring teachers.

You make an interesting point with regard to the "top-down" allegations surrounding standards. Although many people have accused the U.S. Department of Education of being the power behind the standards movement, the truth is that states have been the ones to establish academic standards, rather than the federal government. In most cases, the states use those standards so that teachers, students, and parents can have a clear understanding of what is expected. State tests, if based on those standards, are not a mystery, but contain questions that are directly related to what students have learned in school. It is true that some teachers and schools have grown accustomed to creating their own curriculum and teaching the units in which they are personally interested. The application of standards requires that teachers modify some of those units if they are not related to the state academic content standards.

The Practicality Factor

Q 4 **How can you focus exclusively on standards without ignoring the human factor and emotional intelligence?**

A Your implication that the human side of the equation is essential to academic success is absolutely correct. If I have ever said, written, or otherwise implied that a focus on standards excludes the human dimensions of emotional intelligence, teamwork, self-efficacy, and a host of other interpersonal and intrapersonal issues, then I was wrong.

When I write and talk about the need for "focus," I am not discouraging essential human dynamics in the classroom any more than I am discouraging the arts, physical education, foreign language, or a host of other vital programs that fall outside of the commonly tested academic core. I am, rather, discouraging the extensive use of mind-numbing "favorite units" that have as their sole criteria for existence their popularity with teachers (and many parents and students as well). I've been in elementary classrooms where three hours (no exaggeration, I was there) of prime instruction time were devoted to cutting out paper pumpkins and pasting them on other pieces of paper. The work is boring for the kids, has zero academic content, and is far more formulaic than creative. Frankly, I don't think this is rare.

Dr. Mike Schmoker (1999), author of the best-selling *Results: The Key to Continuous Improvement* and a nationally known expert on improving student achievement, has found examples of such a lack of focus. He reports that only a tiny percentage of the hundreds of elementary classrooms he has visited in the past two years have had reading instruction going on at the time that the principal and teachers had agreed that reading would be the focus. Crafts (not art), dittos, and projects without purpose prevail in far too many classrooms. I'm not trying to endorse a scripted approach or suppress all freedom and creativity, but I don't think it's asking too much of any teacher to relate the activity at hand to what students are expected to learn that year. In sum, properly applied standards create a framework within which much creativity can abound. But the framework also creates boundaries that most teachers, parents, and school leaders can agree are a balance between anarchy and micromanagement.

5 How can all students be judged with the same expectations?

This question appears to presume that the only accurate answer would be, "Of course we can't judge all students with the same expectations; it's obvious that students come to us with widely varying backgrounds and they should be judged accordingly." The presumption may have an element of truth, but is ultimately wrong. While it is true that many students come to school ill-prepared for the challenges ahead of them, this lack of preparation must not form the basis for low expectations by teachers and administrators. The duty of education is more than the mere validation of the knowledge students had before they entered the schoolhouse door. Our job is to make a difference, and that obligation is not diminished by the fact that many students come to our classrooms with less than ideal preparation. A fundamental principle of the standards-based classroom is consistent expectations and standards for all students. This consistency does not diminish the wide variation among students nor does it prevent an honest appraisal of those differences. Rather, the differences among students should lead to variations in teaching strategies and time allocation, not to variations in expectations.

6 How do you really put the standards model into practice? It sounds like pure theory and philosophy.

Standards are not "pure theory and philosophy." I understand your skepticism, but the facts are clear. Standards have had a dramatic and positive impact on student achievement in schools across the nation. By establishing clear expectations of what students should know and be able to do, standards create fairness and an opportunity to learn for all students. If fairness is a "theory," then I suppose it is fair to use that term to apply to standards. But the theory also has a practical application, including an impact on the curriculum and assessment in the classroom.

So how do we build a bridge from "theory and philosophy" to actual practice? My book, *Making Standards Work* (2002), provides ten steps to creating standards-based performance assessments, and it also contains several appendices with practical ideas for creating a standards-based classroom and school. Here is a summary of some critical steps to put standards into practice:

1. *Read* the state and district standards that apply to your classroom and school. There is no substitute for reading them and thinking about how they apply to your curriculum. I have never encountered a case in which the standards are perfectly matched to the textbooks and curriculum that teachers have been given. That means that educators have the obligation to think about what is missing in the current curriculum and, more importantly, what units are in the current curriculum that can be eliminated.

2. *Prioritize* the standards. Every state has published standards; few have taken the essential step of distinguishing the "power standards" from the mass of good ideas that teachers might complete if they had a 400-day school year and students with photographic memories. Frankly, I don't think that most states will ever take this step of prioritization, so it is essential that educators at the school and district level do so. We know, for example, that number operations are important for every 4th grader, but mastering the rhombus and ellipse probably isn't necessary to advance to the 5th grade. When we're short on time and students need to focus, we need to know what our priorities are.

3. *Select* (and, if necessary, *create*) *assessments* that match the standards. How do I know if a standard has been met? Only when the student has provided evidence of proficiency. The average of grades in a grade book and the cryptic marks on a report card rarely tell me if a student is proficient. This is the teacher's judgment based on the preponderance of evidence gathered over time.

4. *Select curriculum* necessary to support student proficiency. This step is in marked contrast to creating lesson plans that match unrealistic and over-burned curricula or the more primitive march through textbooks until, inevitably, we run out of gas in the spring. The selection of a standards-based curriculum implies focus, discernment, and the clear exclusion of many things that are now in textbooks, lesson plans, and curricula. An effective standards-based curriculum is planned "with the end in mind." That's why

you complete step 3, assessment design, before you address step 4, the selection of the curriculum.

5. *Collaborate* with colleagues with a focus on real student work. Collaboration is at the heart of effective standards implementation. The profession of education is not solitary. That is the fallacy of those who implore school leaders to "just close the door and let me teach." Ours is inherently a collaborative profession, and the implementation of standards-based assessment and curriculum requires the development of a consensus on what "proficiency" in meeting a standard really means. This also allows professionals to engage in frequent mid-course corrections so that we can improve teaching, learning, curriculum, assessment, and leadership.

Standards Versus Standardization

7 Is it safe to say that a fair standards system is one that addresses the next step for an individual student? This would make standards dynamic and acceptable to developmental values, and to democratic values. I disagree with the values packages that use uniform standards as a mechanism of exclusion, leading to an educational walled community.

The heart of the question is this: Must the use of standards lead to standardization? The answer is emphatically no. Within the framework of academic standards, there is an extraordinary degree of freedom for teachers to meet the needs of individual students by pursuing standards through different strategies, with alternative paces and styles of learning. These different strategies, however, must not lead to differences in expectation. In fact, if we wish to pursue the democratic values noted in your question, then we must have a commitment to the principle that all students have the opportunity to meet the same high standards.

Although many people endorse individualization of instruction, we must be quite wary if that leads to vastly different expectations of students based on their backgrounds. In the language of your question, the "next step" must be individualized. But the ultimate objective of proficiency in meeting the standards remains the same for all of our students. We can learn a great deal from our colleagues in special education. They routinely deal with students with widely varying learning backgrounds, and, thus, they must individualize instruction accordingly. Yet all special educators work on intellectual and life skills standards that will enrich the lives of their students, understanding all the while that the paths to these standards will vary widely. In other words, effective educators can embrace standards while rejecting standardization.

Q

8 Can there really be the same standards between teachers? Everyone's perceptions are different.

A It is not only possible, but necessary. When every teacher has a different standard, students are left thinking that there is really no such thing as good writing and complete work in math, but only "what Mrs. Jones wants." Although teachers may not agree on everything, surely we can agree on a few fundamentals. We can agree, for example, on what good informative writing is. We can agree on what a good science lab report looks like. We can agree on what a complete math problem should be. We already have agreements on discipline, safety, immunizations, and even the rules of basketball and playground games. Can't we find a way to agree on some academic requirements that are at least as important as those things on which we already agree?

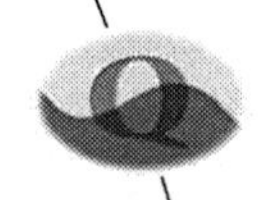

9 How do you establish school-based standards?

Schools need not establish standards from scratch. In the U.S., every state except Iowa has created academic content standards, although every district in Iowa has them. Overseas, many nations have created national standards, and there are abundant models of academic content standards to consider if your school is either independent or in a nation without established academic content standards. You can find numerous examples of standards at our web site, www.LeadandLearn.com.

As you establish standards, the heart of the matter is addressing the central question, "What do students need to know and be able to do?" At the state policy level, that can lead to statements of standards that are unclear, unfocused, and unhelpful. So let's consider the heart of your question: How do we establish standards at the *school* level?

The heart of school-based standards implementation is a focus on student work. That means looking at an assessment, the scoring guide (or rubric), and a piece of student work (without the name), and then evaluating it. First, each teacher evaluates it alone; then with a colleague. Then, collaborate in larger groups. These conversations may lead to clarifications and constructive changes in the rubric or in the student instructions. The conversations may also reveal implicit expectations by teachers that cause different evaluations for no apparent reasons.

How can we communicate these expectations to all students? Think of how we approach discipline and behavior. We don't have the entire school board disciplinary policy posted in every classroom, nor do we spend time at faculty meetings discussing every paragraph of the disciplinary policy. Rather, we focus on those few behavior issues that we know are most important to the creation and maintenance of a safe and orderly environment. So it is with standards. We need not discuss and review every single standard, only those that all teachers have in common: writing, problem-solving, and critical thinking.

10 How can teachers incorporate standards into their everyday instruction? In other words, how can a teacher teach standards in informative, meaningful ways?

First, teachers have an obligation to make their expectations clear *before* they assign work to students. This is the heart and soul of a standards-based approach to teaching. Second, teachers in a standards-based environment have an obligation to ask this question of every classroom activity: Is this use of classroom time helping my students to meet the academic content standards of my state? A careful response to this question would eliminate an enormous amount of activity in many classrooms that are familiar to the teacher but that are essentially wasteful of time and energy. Third, teachers in a standards-based classroom insist that their feedback must be respected. Teacher feedback is respected only when students use it to improve performance. This means that teacher evaluation is not the "final word" in assessing student performance, but is rather a means to improve student performance. The teacher is a coach, not merely an evaluator. The teacher is a guide, not merely an instructor. In sum, standards provide better information, better performance, and more encouragement for students. Standards provide more respect for teachers and more information for parents.

11 A colleague of mine recently showed me a document you wrote called a "Standards Implementation Checklist." Can you tell me more about it?

The Standards Implementation Checklist was originally created for my book, *Making Standards Work* (2002), but can be found here in Appendix A. There are three checklists: one for classrooms, one for buildings, and one for the district. The focus of all of these checklists is the implementation of standards to improve student achievement.

Although you are welcome to modify and use them however you would like, let me offer two suggestions for you and your colleagues to consider:

1. Identify those areas of standards implementation where you are already doing an exceptionally good job. It is important to recognize that you are building on a strong foundation in your district and not starting from scratch.

2. Identify one or two areas for particular focus in the next 2-3 months. It might be, for example, the creation of just one standards-based performance assessment. It might be the use of a faculty meeting or other forum to focus on student work and allow a colleague to evaluate your students' work. My experience suggests that when schools attempt to implement many different goals simultaneously, few if any of them receive serious attention. Therefore, I encourage you to focus on a very few—perhaps four or five—of the checklist items that are most helpful for you and your students.

12 Can you provide examples of how to display standards within the classroom? Do they remain up all year or change as the curriculum rolls out? How detailed should they be?

The display of standards in a classroom contains two elements: a description of the work and an example of proficient student work. The description of work is typically in the form of a scoring guide, or "rubric." This is a description, in student language, of work at all levels of achievement, including work that is exemplary, proficient, progressing, and not meeting standards. The example of proficient student work need not be taken from students in the class. Indeed, many teachers find that the use of "model" work from a student in the class creates confusion because students have a difficult time analyzing the quality of the work without thinking about the identity of the student who created it. Thus, the use of anonymous "model" work helps students to focus on work quality and what an academic standard means in practice.

The idea of posting a standard is hardly new. Teachers almost always have some standards posted—standards for behavior, homework, and other "class rules." An early elementary class might have standards clearly posted for handwriting and the labeling of papers all year, while a high school science class might have the standards for the composition of a lab report posted all year. Other standards displays might be changed throughout the year, as projects and assignments change.

Q 13 **Some of my teachers in first grade have come to me very concerned about students who were listed as proficient in kindergarten and are now being measured against a standard that places that same student at basic or below. I have reminded them that they are now measuring students against a standard and not another set of students. I continue to remind them that this is new to all of us in our district and in the state. I tell them to collaborate with each other and to team together to fill those needs. What other suggestions might you have for them and me?**

A First, a standards-based system is indeed more rigorous than a norm-based system. Simply "beating" other kids in a sample isn't enough. Students must demonstrate proficiency compared to an objective standard. That's the most fair and effective way to help students learn.

Second, it is a real tragedy when a child is told in the early primary grades that everything is just fine, only to face a 4th grade test that, after years of public education, labels the child as "not proficient." Learning that we need to work on some areas in first grade is great. That sort of feedback and guidance is an essential part of effective education. Unfortunately, if students learn of their needs for improvement only after several years in school (perhaps in the 4th grade or, more tragically, in secondary school), then we have failed in our fundamental debt of honesty to students. Some teachers fear that if we tell students in elementary school that they have not yet met a standard, it will hurt their self-esteem. In fact, students love to achieve and do well, and they only can do so if we are honest about where they can improve. The real harm to self-esteem occurs when students reach later grades and find that they are not proficient, and only then realize that no one told them earlier that they needed to work on some essential skills.

In the elementary classroom, there is enormous complexity. Some students can read in kindergarten; other students cannot form their letters properly at the end of first grade. Does this acknowledgment that students didn't enter first grade meeting standards render a negative judgment on kindergarten teachers? Certainly not. The official "Reeves canon of kindergarten instruction" consists of 1) loving school; 2) learning to attend to the teacher; 3) respecting other kids; and 4) when in doubt, return to #1. It is, however, important to be completely candid and honest with students and parents about what kids can and cannot do.

Consider the central question of assessment and learning: Why, after all, do we assess student performance compared to a standard? If the answer is merely that we must have a system for evaluation and grading (or, worse yet, that we must have a basis for humiliation, embarrassment, ranking, and sorting), then I can understand the feelings of frustration and anger expressed by some teachers. But that is an inadequate response to the question. Why do we assess students? The one and only purpose of assessment is the improvement of student learning. Every bit of feedback is friendly, helpful, and necessary. The observation that a student is not meeting a first grade standard in the fall is accurate, normal, and helpful, particularly since I know that your teachers would not regard this observation as a permanent condition of the child. It's just an observation, like taking a temperature or noting that a child needs a vaccination. It's not judgmental, just a statement of fact.

The most important question for every educator and administrator to ask right now is this: What am I doing differently now and what will I do differently in the next two months based on my observations of my students' strengths and challenges over the past two months?

I know that your teachers will move beyond hearing standards as negative judgments and toward using them as a tool for learning, coaching, and encouragement. Whenever a student doesn't meet a standard, your teachers' consistent rejoinder is "yet" as they maintain the high standard, but give students multiple opportunities to learn. That, along with healthy doses of love, encouragement, and coaching, will make this a terrific year.

Standards for All?

14 How can I balance high expectations with developmentally appropriate practice?

First, let's define "developmentally appropriate practice." This phrase has been terribly distorted to connote low expectations when its etymology was precisely the opposite. Developmentally appropriate practice means recognizing the cognitive and neurological abilities of the students. That often means *higher* expectations, not lower. The association of "developmentally appropriate practice" with lower expectations is simply inaccurate, whether we're talking about early childhood development, 3rd graders struggling with a multi-step math problem, or 8th graders dealing with algebra. In fact, observations of children at play make it clear that we can expect great complexity and challenge: more complexity and challenge than many advocates of "developmentally appropriate practice" would acknowledge. Thus, it is *not* a "balance" of high expectations with developmentally appropriate practice. In fact, the latter inevitably leads to the former. The fact that a student has a different background or some learning deprivation does not indicate that it is "developmentally inappropriate" to give that student the gift of high expectations and exceptional challenge.

15 Is it fair to the children with low IQs to be expected to score above their ability on the achievement test?

We must first be clear about the label of "low IQ" really means. If the low cognitive ability of students requires them to participate in an Individualized Education Plan (IEP), then they are expected to meet their IEP objectives; they are not necessarily expected to "score above their ability" on tests. However, there are many children who may have been labeled with a "low IQ"—that is, they process information more slowly than other children according to some tests—but these children have no neurological or cognitive impairments. They're just normal kids who don't process information as quickly as other kids. For these students, it is absolutely fair to expect them to score well; indeed, it is imperative that teachers maintain these expectations. Without high expectations, these students will confirm what they have probably been told many times on the playground and elsewhere: they are slow; they are "dummies." The profession of teaching is based on the premise that we can successfully intervene in these cases. These kids are essentially normal and capable, but need extra help, confidence, work, and encouragement.

16 What do we do with kids who don't meet standards? Is there a specialized path to follow?

There are two reasons a student might not meet standards. The first is that the student has a cognitive impairment, and then they are subject to the Individualized Education Plan. The IEP takes precedence over everything else for those students—it's a matter of federal law. Teachers measure the extent to which the students meet their IEP objectives and report that accurately to parents.

There are many students, however, who have no cognitive impairment, but who still do not meet state standards. These students need intensive intervention and, in many cases, they need more time. If a student comes to 4th grade reading at the

2nd grade level, it is unfair to the 4th grade teacher to expect that this student will achieve standards unless we specifically provide for intervention for that student. Successful intervention programs could include not only the traditional programs, such as summer school and additional after-school help, but also intensive interventions during the school day.

Following are some intensive intervention models. For more on intervention, consult Chapter 7, "Interventions for Underperforming Students."

1. *Double Math and Double Literacy*. Students take double periods of math and literacy. For instance, in addition to the regular algebra class, the student would also take "Algebra Methods." Or, in addition to a regular language arts class, the student would also take "Technical Writing."

2. *Intensive Training*. At the beginning of the school year, the student spends 30-40 days working on intensive academics, organization, and behavior. Many students who came to school without adequate preparation will be working at grade level by the end of this program.

3. *WIN (Work In Now) Model*. At a high school in Wisconsin, one assistant principal became the "Academic Dean." When any student missed one assignment, they were referred to the Dean. The Dean demands 100% homework 100% of the time. The teachers don't have to hassle with the behavior and discipline problems that skipped or late homework entails. The teacher is no longer the "bad guy." The high school experienced a reduction of more than 120 student course failures, saving time and money for the school, and reducing lost opportunities by the students.

CHAPTER

2

Standardized Tests

Standardized Tests: Boon or Bane?

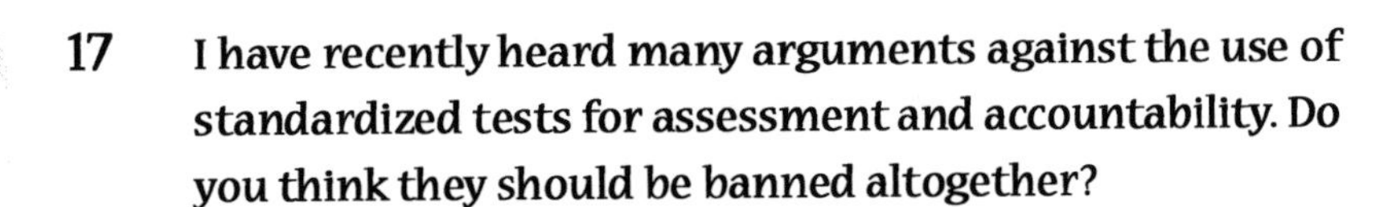

17 I have recently heard many arguments against the use of standardized tests for assessment and accountability. Do you think they should be banned altogether?

I am certainly no apologist for standardized tests or the testing companies. Indeed, I have written a number of critical comments about standardized tests. See, for example, the first part of my book, *Making Standards Work* (2002). That said, let's acknowledge what standardized tests can and cannot do. These tests can provide a brief and limited snapshot of student knowledge in particular areas. They can also compare the responses of one student to a group of other students on the same question or group of questions. What these tests can never do is measure a broad concept such as "educational quality" of schools and teachers, and the tests certainly do not measure the general knowledge of students. In the best accountability systems, standardized test scores are used as one of many indicators. Moreover, the best standardized tests allow students to "show what they know," not only in a multiple choice format but also through short answers and more extensive written work products. For two views of the limitations and strengths of standardized tests, consider two recent books. Popham's *Testing! Testing!: What Every Parent Should Know About School Tests* (1999) is a critical review of the weaknesses of standardized tests. Schmoker's *Results: The Key to Continuous School Improvement* (1999) acknowledges that while standardized tests cannot be the sole indicator of educational quality, these instruments do provide an essential focus for educators and school leaders.

18 What is the difference between a norm-referenced test and a criterion-referenced test?

A norm-referenced test provides results that compare the score of one student to the scores of students in a sample that purportedly represents students throughout the nation (the so-called "norming" group). Results are frequently provided using percentiles, quartiles, or other comparative numbers that tell the reader how a student performed compared to the norming group. For example, it might show that a student scored "better than 55% of students in a comparison group of other 5th graders."

A criterion-referenced test provides results that compare the score of each student to a standard of proficiency rather than to other students. This provides quite different reports to parents and the community. In a norm-referenced test, students are typically quite satisfied to be "above average," that is, better than 50% of the students in a comparison group. Such a comparison does not tell the student or any other observer of the data anything about the competence of the student, just that the student is a little more competent (or a little less incompetent) than the average.

There is an important difference between these two approaches to testing. In many states using criterion-referenced tests, there has been terrible publicity surrounding a statement such as "80% of students do not meet the standards!" Amidst the wailing and gnashing of teeth surrounding these headlines there is a little noticed fact: Had the state taken a norm-referenced approach to testing, the headline would have blared "49.9% of students are above average!," a claim that could have been mathematically accurate without spending a penny of state funds or a moment of student time on a test.

Q 19 **How long do we, as classroom teachers, re-teach a concept before we move on to the next concept? If grasping a concept is our first priority, then why have timed tests like the Stanford 9?**

A The standards clearly refer to achievement, not merely to speed. Nevertheless, for a host of practical reasons, most tests and performances have some time limits. But every coach and music teacher knows the maxim that "proficiency precedes speed," and yet every coach and music teacher prepares their students for a "final" performance. The same is true in academic disciplines. Even if there is a timed test that the students must take in the future, teachers are well advised to concentrate first on proficiency, rather than pace, of student performance. We can focus on fewer standards by considering the use of "power standards": that small subset of standards that is really necessary for student success. We know that literacy, mathematical computation, and problem-solving ability, as well as time management and organization, are necessary for students to have success in secondary school. It may help you to take a glance at the list of Power Standards for Middle Schools at the back of this book in Appendix B.

With regard to the issue of "how long" you wait, let's ask a fundamental question: "How do we know that a student cannot do a task?" The mere failure of a student to do it may have more to do with organization and work ethic than a lack of ability. The response by a teacher and administrator might be more productive if it involves restricted choice, more work, or a changed curriculum. All of these are more effective than giving a student a low grade for unsatisfactory work. This is a "punishment" that has no practical impact and, for the student, might even be a reward if the result is that the assignment was not really necessary for passing the class.

Getting the Data You Need

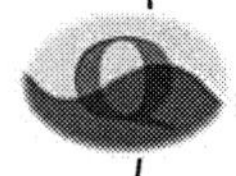

20 When will we use something other than standardized test scores to measure student achievement?

A How about tomorrow? There is nothing in the law of any state that prohibits classrooms, schools, and districts from reporting more than their standardized test scores. Many districts already use locally created assessments, teacher judgments, and other criteria in their public reporting. We may not be able to avoid standardized tests, but we need not be solely dependent on them as the only indicator of student achievement. Every school and district has the power to use additional measurements.

21 Considering that my school is a 7th and 8th grade school, are year-to-year comparisons valid given the fact that half (about 600) of the students are new? How could I best use the data?

As you note, year-to-year comparisons of standardized test scores tell you nothing about individual students unless you are comparing the score of the *same* students. However, these year-to-year comparisons can be *very* useful in analyzing curriculum. In fact, the very reason that the multi-year comparisons are not good for analyzing individual student performance (the use of different kids) is what makes them so effective in analyzing curriculum. If the same sub-scale differences are apparent with *different* kids, then you know that the differential is not the result of a unique group of students, but is very likely the result of curriculum, teaching, texts, misalignment, or other non-student variables. On Stanford 9, for example, one of the most frequent sub-scale differences I see is the presence of strong calculation and geometry scores, accompanied by weak performances in problem solving and measurement. When the same sub-scale differences occur with many different groups of students in the same school, then it tells me that the teachers have something to work on. Using that example (check your own data; I wouldn't be surprised to see the same sub-scale differences in your school), it would suggest that we analyze when and how frequently we do problem solving and measurement. Usually the answers are "late" and "infrequently." Scores won't change until teaching and curriculum change. This implies that we need to enlist the support of colleagues in physical education, art, music, science, and social studies to assist in very specific ways to improve student measurement and problem-solving skills. For more information on using test scores to improve instruction and achievement, see Chapter 3 on Performance Assessments and Chapter 8 on Accountability.

22 A teacher wants to use a standardized test (the California Achievement Test) as a pretest in October and a posttest in April. It will be the same exact test given both times and to the same students. Would giving the test in October and then giving the exact same test in April invalidate the score in April because the students have seen the test six months earlier?

I respectfully disagree with the assessment technique you have described on several counts.

First, the authors and owners of the test themselves have stated emphatically that the use you describe is inappropriate for this test. It is no more than a "snapshot" of a limited part of the curriculum and not a comprehensive view of student achievement. Even if a different form of the test were used in the spring, the same problem would present itself: You would be drawing too great an inference from a single assessment instrument.

Second, the standardized test you described relies exclusively on multiple choice methodology. With a choice of five responses, this allows for a 20% random error rate and the accompanying "false positives" (that is, guessing correctly one out of five times, telling parents and the public that a student knows the answer when this is not the case). I have no quarrel with some use of multiple choice tests, but their *exclusive* use to describe student achievement or progress is inappropriate.

Third, April is a bit late to find out that students are not making acceptable progress. A far better assessment and accountability system includes frequent intermediate indicators. Thus, student, teacher, and parents can make appropriate "mid-course corrections" rather than simply finding out about failures late in the school year. Moreover, anyone, including children terrorized by tests and adults who have had a bad day, can blow a test now and then. Relying on a single instrument for a couple of hours to label "student achievement" is akin to relying on a single measurement of body temperature to indicate health. Hospitals measure vital signs frequently and they measure them in many different ways. Schools could learn from that approach.

23 How do you set benchmarks using norm-referenced tests? My curriculum department wants to use "Below Grade Level" data, but I don't know how to obtain that information from a norm-referenced test. I'm hesitant to compile data using a Grade Equivalent cutoff. Is it only possible to create benchmarks using criterion-referenced tests?

I understand that people want test data to provide clear and unambiguous information. As we both know, it's difficult to take the complex subject of student achievement and reduce it to a simple binary (on or off grade level) system. With that caution, let me offer some ideas for your consideration.

First, norm-referenced data are emphatically *not* the same as grade-level data. People who use it that way sometimes assume that the 50th percentile is the same as being "on grade level." That doesn't tell you anything about achievement of your state's standards for a grade level, but only how the student fares compared to other students.

Second, norm-referenced results can offer valuable information if you use them as a part of a comprehensive assessment picture. For example, a student might be deemed to be "proficient" in mathematics if that student meets three or four of the following criteria:

- 70% correct on the state math assessment items (note: not 70th percentile, but 70% correct. Use the raw scores).
- "Proficient" or better on a district math performance assessment, evaluated by the classroom teacher or team of teachers (this can be administered more than once).
- "Proficient" or better on an independent assessment (i.e., by someone other than the student's classroom teacher) of math portfolio contents.

- 70% or more correct on a district-administered criterion-referenced multiple choice test.

This system allows a student to meet your grade level standards even if they have a bad day on the norm-referenced test. Similarly, it allows a student who has a run-in with a teacher but otherwise does well in math to meet your standards. This will work better than putting all of your evaluation eggs in the norm-referenced testing basket.

Surviving the Testing Process

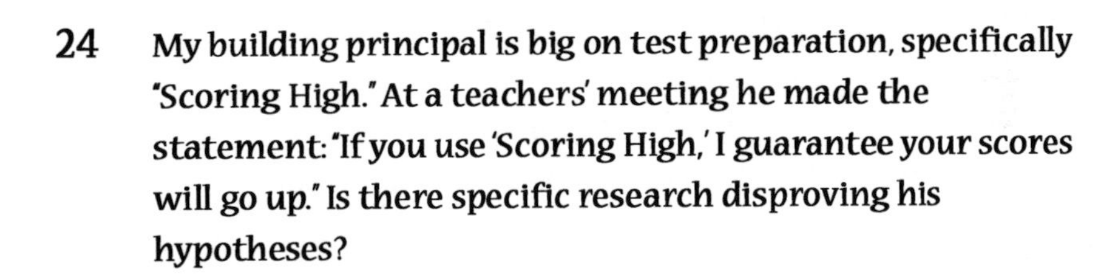

24 My building principal is big on test preparation, specifically "Scoring High." At a teachers' meeting he made the statement: "If you use 'Scoring High,' I guarantee your scores will go up." Is there specific research disproving his hypotheses?

I'm not familiar with "Scoring High" or the research surrounding it. I can only hope that the company that sold it can offer some research to support their claims. After all, the burden of proof is on them to validate the claims and not on others to disprove their hypotheses. What we do know for certain is this:

1. Test scores may be politically important, and we may want kids to do well on them, but test items are not the only thing that students must learn.
2. Classical test prep relies on item familiarization; that is, practicing items in class similar to those on the test. That is useful to a very limited point: It lets the teachers know who knows the answers and who doesn't. But it doesn't tell the teacher *why* the students don't know the answers. If test prep really is useful, it should lead to effective teaching strategies, improved learning, and then higher test scores.

3. A combination of written responses with traditional test prep is a better balance than test prep alone. If students focus on informative writing, then not only will students have the knowledge they need for the test, but the teacher will gain much better insight into how to help students. Moreover, students will have more skills than merely responding to multiple choice questions, and they will have a skill that endures far beyond the day the test is administered. At the very least, you can incorporate some writing into the test prep. Examples of how to do this include asking students to provide written explanations for *why* two of the wrong answers are incorrect. It takes longer, but gives both student and teacher much more value than mere test prep.

25 I have had reports of teachers helping students during testing. My personal feeling is that this practice is growing as teachers feel the pressure to produce improvement in their students' academic achievement. Any insight you can provide as to how to combat the problem would be very much appreciated. I would very much like to hear what measures other school districts employ to keep students and teachers from bending the rules. Gone unchecked, and finally discovered, this could be the undoing of any progress we make.

The situation you describe is serious. However well-intentioned, such "helping" is destructive for both the student and the ethic of academic progress. Students must understand the difference between feedback from teachers on in-progress projects and cheating. The simple solution I would propose (and have already used in many districts) is that teachers be randomly assigned to other classes on test days. This is as much for the protection of teachers as for the testing process. With such random assignment, no one can accuse teachers of cheating. Think of what happens when someone has a legitimate increase in test scores? The eyes of the skeptics

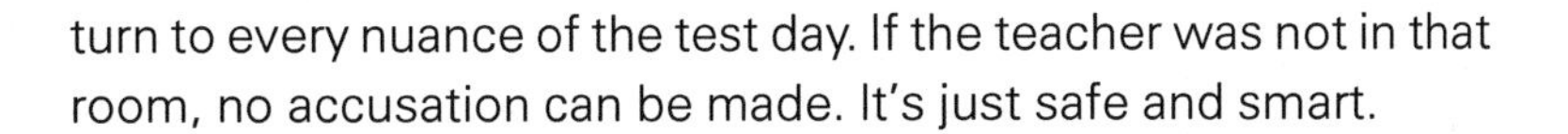
turn to every nuance of the test day. If the teacher was not in that room, no accusation can be made. It's just safe and smart.

26 I have heard it said that when teachers try to raise students' test scores, they abandon all good teaching practices and the students must abandon thinking and reasoning skills. But standardized tests are a "necessary evil." How can I help my kids do better without turning their minds to mush?

This argument is a debate of two inappropriate extremes. At one end of the rhetorical continuum is the contention that standardized tests (preferably in multiple choice format) are the only right way to measure student achievement and school success. Only with the threat of purely objective tests will teachers and students be "whipped into shape." The other extreme holds that tests are inherently evil, particularly when they originate outside of the classroom. The very existence of these externally imposed tests forces otherwise level-headed teachers and students to become bumbling piles of intellectual rubble, prevented by the tests from exercising thinking and communicative skills or engaging in effective teaching practice.

Neither extreme is supported by the evidence. If the first extreme were true, the schools with the highest quantity of testing with the highest stakes would have the most capable students and teachers. The 1998 results of the National Assessment of Educational Progress appear to suggest otherwise (find their results on the web at www.nces.ed.gov). In Linda Darling-Hammond's wonderful turn of phrase, there is little evidence to suggest that weighing the cow more frequently makes it fatter.

If the second extreme were true, the schools with standardized tests—particularly those schools that show progress with improved test scores—should be devoid of any activities save mindless test drills. Interdisciplinary instruction, performance assessment, critical reasoning, and writing should all have gone the way of Socrates. This view is also unsupported by the evidence. If the "testing = bad teaching" and "testing = no thinking or writing" hypotheses were true, one should find at least a few instances of negative relationships between test scores and writing (measured either by proficiency in writing or frequency of writing assessment). Despite a surfeit of rhetoric alleging the truth of this hypothesis, our research in many states in several disciplines from elementary through secondary school fail to confirm the "testing = bad teaching" hypothesis. In fact, the evidence suggests that the highest test scores are associated not with mindless test drills, but with more writing assessment and with more interdisciplinary writing.

What does this mean for teachers and school leaders? Whether or not there are standardized tests to be taken, the path to excellence (and, incidentally, to higher scores) is more frequent writing in a variety of different academic disciplines.

CHAPTER

3

Performance Assessment

Getting Started: Implementing Performance Assessment

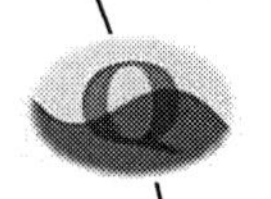

27 What is a performance assessment? How does it differ from other kinds of assessment?

A performance assessment requires a demonstration of knowledge, skills, and understanding by the student. Unlike a multiple-choice test, one cannot guess the correct answer to a performance assessment. Prospective drivers and pilots, for example, must take both a written multiple-choice test and also a performance assessment. The pilot must not only have a theoretical understanding of weather, air traffic control, and navigation, but also must have an equal number of take-offs and landings in order for the Federal Aviation Administration examiner to certify the pilot as proficient. In the context of schools, students who successfully complete a performance assessment must typically demonstrate understanding, perhaps through an experiment or the solution to a problem, and must successfully communicate that understanding, typically through written or oral presentations.

Performance assessments are generally evaluated using scoring guides (commonly called "rubrics"). These documents allow the student to understand precisely what the examiners will regard as "proficient" work. There is neither mystery nor guesswork in the process. Different examiners, all using the same scoring guide, should come to the same or very similar conclusions about the quality of a student's work product.

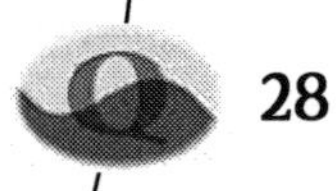

28 I want to start using performance assessments in my school. I think they will be received well by the teachers, but I don't have much time for planning or discussion. How should I lay out the plan? How much time and what type of activities do I need? I just need help getting started.

First, take small, achievable steps. Set short-term deadlines for clearly defined tasks. For instance, you could propose that within the next 30 days, there would be a first draft of a school-wide informative writing rubric or scoring guide. By two weeks after the publication of these drafts, every teacher would have tried to use the scoring guide at least twice. Within the four weeks after that, every teacher would have exchanged at least one set of papers with a colleague. These things can be done in normal meeting and class time, and don't require a great deal of additional time on your part. It will be important to set aside time in faculty meetings to discuss progress and to revise and improve the continuing work.

Second, use models of effective performance assessment. There are many sources for these, such as www.LeadandLearn.com.

Third, identify your faculty leaders for specialized professional development. One of the most important rewards you can offer to your cutting-edge leaders is the opportunity to interact with other leaders across the country.

Fourth, continue to set clear and reasonable goals for the coming year. For example, try asking teachers to measure the extent to which students meet state standards in four or five key areas (such as math problem-solving, informative writing, reading comprehension, science reasoning, and creative writing). Along with each report card, teachers would be expected to report the students' progress on these key indicators and be ready to support that judgment with appropriate assessment information. This is certainly not the ultimate goal of weekly performance assessment, but it represents reasonable moves toward that objective.

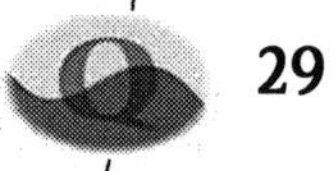

29 How often do the teachers need to be doing assessments? Should there be one for every lesson? Should there be more than one per week?

The time it takes to complete an entire performance assessment will vary based upon the assessment written and the student working on it. Some assessments might take as long as five or six weeks, while other assessments might be finished within one week. As you know, each classroom of students will come to you with different levels of skill and knowledge. The time spent on each assessment becomes fluid.

Here are some things to keep in mind with performance assessments:

1. The more teachers work with performance assessments, the less whole-class instruction will occur. A "lesson" may become introducing the assessment, clarifying instructions, and creating scoring guides. The rest of the time, students work together or on their own and the teacher becomes the coach.

2. The goal with performance assessments is to help all students become proficient at the state standards.

Most performance assessments have at least four tasks. This gives students multiple opportunities to develop the skills and knowledge necessary to meet state standards.

30 As an administrator at an elementary school, I am faced with transferring the information that I learn to my staff. Many see performance assessments as 'glorified lesson plans.' I need help to guide the staff to see that performance assessment means kids will learn more. Please point me in the right direction.

You have touched on a very important point: If teachers think that performance assessment is a "glorified lesson plan," they will be disappointed. They aren't really engaging in performance assessment, so they will not get any of the benefits of it. It is somewhat like teachers who say that they are doing "cooperative learning" and then do little more than unstructured discussions among students. They are, inevitably, disappointed that "cooperative learning doesn't work" when they actually failed to implement cooperative learning in the first place.

So, what does good performance assessment entail? There are three major points:

1. Performance assessment should have an *engaging scenario*. Students need a compelling reason to be involved in the activity.

2. The assessment contains *multiple tasks*. There should be at least four to accommodate the different learning paces and backgrounds of all students in the class.

3. The assessment involves *intermediate feedback*. Teachers do not wait until the entire assessment is completed to make a final evaluation, but instead provide feedback and midcourse corrections throughout the activity.

The fundamental purpose of performance assessment is the improvement of student learning, not the rendering of an evaluation. Moreover, performance assessment need not be done at the exclusion of traditional tests. We favor a balanced approach in which teachers use traditional tests (multiple choice and essay) for periodic monitoring of what students know. But the majority of assessment should be formative: used not to give a grade, but to learn what students know, how teaching should be adjusted, and to improve student skills.

Q **31** **We believe in giving students multiple opportunities to prove themselves, as opposed to success or failure on the first and only try. The problem is our tradition of "one-shot" tests. Parents and students have been comfortable with this, and many are not comfortable with "multiple opportunities to learn" in our standards-based system. How can we get the true message out about performance assessments?**

A There is no doubt that your decision to provide "multiple opportunities" for students will challenge some traditional notions of testing. I think that you should stand firm on this because it is the right thing to do. Therefore, let's consider how to have a constructive dialog with parents about the change from "one-shot" tests to "multiple opportunities." If you provide students with "multiple opportunities to learn," you will have the parents of those kids who "got it the first time" very upset with you. But consider this: We routinely expect wide differences in the pace of students, with appropriately differentiated instructional strategies, for our football teams. Does every player do the same play at the "proficient" level the first time? Probably not. What happened when a player was not proficient? Did the coach give him a "D" in the Left Reverse? Rather unlikely. The players who were not proficient the first time ran the play again, and again, and again. In other words, the football teams on which we lavish the most sophisticated instructional strategies routinely receive "multiple opportunities to learn." But if you try that in a math class, you may face some disgruntled parents and teachers. I'm not asking for much, just that we take reading, writing, and mathematics as seriously as we take football. Try these explanations with parents and teachers who remain advocates of one-shot testing. These arguments may not satisfy them, but the job of the leader is not to satisfy everyone with a complaint. The leader's job is to do the right thing and, with great respect, care, and explanation, implement the best policies and strategies for the school.

32 I am an elementary teacher interested in finding some information on culturally fair assessments. Can you help?

First, let's address the issue of cultural fairness. One way to determine item bias in a test is to compare the responses of one group of students who are equally adept in a subject to another group of students. If the results on an item vary substantially, then one may speculate that it was the item context, not the content, that accounted for the difference in equally able students.

Does this mean that we can never include a cultural context in test questions? Certainly not. Students must deal with different contexts in literature, social studies, science, and mathematics, not to mention real life, all the time. Therefore, it is not necessarily "culturally biased" to use a game, such as soccer, baseball, lacrosse or mah-jongg, in a math test, provided that the students are evaluated on their ability to solve the math problem and not on their prior knowledge of the rules of those games. In order to remove cultural bias, one need not remove all cultural references. Rather, the teacher must remove the dependence of the student on prior cultural knowledge. You can achieve this, in the examples above, by careful explanations of the rules to those games and through the use of games from a variety of cultures so that students are not advantaged or disadvantaged based on their previous cultural knowledge.

Possible Roadblocks

33 If students take 5 or 6 tries to complete a project up to a standard, how can we deal with classroom management if we have 3 or 4 different projects with different materials happening in one 45 minute period?

A This is perfectly normal. Surely there are not classrooms full of clones who all work on the same task and finish it at precisely the same time. Orchestras and football teams routinely have students working on 3 or 4 different things at the same time in the same 45-minute period. Academic classes can do the same. We engage in fantasy when we think that because we are in front of the group speaking in whole-group instruction, every student is really learning and doing the same thing. We should plan assessments and assignments with the knowledge that students will be doing different tasks at the same time, and completing tasks at different times.

34 How can I measure learning if my schedule is based on time?

A First, let's consider the premise of your question. Schedules are, by nature, "based on time," but that does not mean that we are incapable of being flexible to meet the needs of students. For example, at the elementary level, teachers across the country are routinely expanding the amount of time they devote to reading from the traditional 60 minutes to as long as three or four hours. At the secondary level, students who need a better foundation in literacy are receiving an extra period or two of literacy so that their opportunities for success are increased. Just because we have a schedule does not mean that we cannot modify the curriculum and course schedules of individual students to meet their needs.

Q 35 Should all teachers in each grade level in our city teach the same performance assessment on the same day in the same way?

A I've seen a number of different successful methods for coordinating assessments without necessarily identifying a specific time and date for the same assessments. There is probably a reasonable middle ground here. On the one hand, the district and state have a reasonable interest in knowing the progress of students. Thus, the expectation that all students take the same (or at least similar) assessments during a specific time frame makes sense. On the other hand, the reality of the classroom and school day is that it is very hard to assume that an identical time slot makes sense for everyone. The usual reason for a common time administration is "test security," but performance assessments are not secret. Anyone can look at them and study them. More preparation will probably provide better performance; that's the way it should work.

You might consider a discussion with the curriculum director and colleagues that would create a "window" of time that meets the district's need for information and also meets the teachers' and principals' needs for flexibility.

Q 36 Some teachers I work with are unclear about whether to teach a lesson before doing a performance assessment. What can I tell them when they say, "My kids don't know this stuff yet"?

With performance assessments, the assessment is the lesson. Assessment becomes curriculum. Standards, curriculum, instruction, and assessment are no longer four separate entities. Rather, curriculum and instruction become a part of the assessment to help students achieve proficiency in standards.

Remember, the fundamental purpose of assessment is to improve student learning. Remind your colleagues that an effective performance assessment teaches the students while they are being assessed. If the first task of an assessment asks students to do things they don't know how to do, then give them the tools to learn. Perhaps students will use the Internet, or magazines, or textbooks. There is no way to really know what kids know and understand until they are assessed.

37 Do all assessments need to be interdisciplinary?

As a general rule, both teachers and students are better served when they work on a smaller number of assessments, with each assessment richer in content. An assessment that is "rich in content" typically addresses more than one discipline. For example, a science assessment considers not only the student's ability to conduct an experiment but the proficiency with which the lab report is written and the accuracy with which the data are arranged in a table and graph. A social studies assessment considers not only proficiency in history or geography but also in reading, writing, and analysis.

For some examples of interdisciplinary assessments, please see the appendices to *Making Standards Work* (Reeves, 2002), or the web site www.LeadandLearn.com.

Scoring and Grading Performance Assessments

38 How do I assign grades in a standards-based system? I have trouble getting away from the percentages. For instance, how do I justify a 2 versus a 3 to parents? How do I translate grades for things like spelling tests and math worksheets? It is easier with more subjective assessments like creative writing.

Let's begin by asking the purpose of grades and report cards. In my view, student-reporting systems (typically in the form of report cards and letter grades) should meet two criteria. First, they should be accurate; they describe what a student can and cannot do. Second, they should be helpful; they give some insight to students, parents, and teachers about how a student can improve. I have never once seen a system composed only of letter grades that meets these criteria. While letter grades may be a practical and political necessity in most schools, they cannot stand alone as accurate descriptions of student work, and they never, announced as isolated symbols, help a student understand how to get better. Fortunately, standards-based grading systems allow parents, students, and teachers a way to make sense of grades.

Let's start with the issue of accuracy. A grade that is accurate will describe what the student can and cannot do. If Alexander receives an "A" in geometry, I should be able to assume that he is proficient or better in that subject. If he receives a "C" in geometry, I should be able to assume that he is passing the class, but also gather that he has not come close to meeting all of the teacher's expectations (that is, the standards) in that class. If he fails the class, it should be clear that he is neither proficient nor is he making progress toward proficiency. Although this is little more than a common sense inference of what letter grades should mean, the actual practice of letter grades falls short of this "common sense" standard. In actual fact, proficient students can receive low grades and non-proficient students can receive "C's" and "B's."

In the traditional system, Jamie receives a "C" even though he is not remotely close to achieving the standard. Nevertheless, he has worked hard and the teacher wants to encourage him with the high grade of "C." Julia, by contrast, receives a "C" even though she is quite advanced in every academic area of the class. Julia is, however, disorganized and uncooperative, her homework is late and slovenly, and the teacher wishes to "get her attention" through the low grade of "C." What does the "C" really mean? It's anyone's guess if the only feedback the students and parents receive is a letter grade.

There is a better way: the standards achievement report. This does not replace the letter grade system, but this report clarifies what the letter grades actually mean. The standards-based report allows teachers to communicate clearly and precisely with students and parents. Jamie is proficient in his worth ethic, but only progressing in his academic knowledge. The report might be even more precise, indicating that Jamie is exceptional in "patterns and shapes" but only progressing in his knowledge of "calculation" and further explain that he is not meeting the standard in "problem-solving." Julia's standards-based report card would indicate with accuracy how capable she is in the academic areas, but would also tell her and her parents that her organization and classroom behavior are not meeting the standard.

If it is necessary to assign a letter grade to these students, then the use of the standards achievement report described in the previous paragraph will, at the very least, let parents understand what the "C" really means.

Standards can be easily translated into grades. Here is one system that teachers have used with success. They create six assessments for each nine-week grading period. Each assessment is rich in content. Perhaps it is a science lab, English theme, geography project, or similarly complex piece of work. Each assessment is graded on a four-point scale: exemplary, proficient, progressing, or not meeting the standard. These are translated to letter grades in the table that follows:

Exemplary	Proficient	Progressing	Not Meeting Standard	Grade
4 Assessments	2 Assessments			A
	4 Assessments	2 Assessments		B
	3 Assessments	3 Assessments		C

If the student is proficient on fewer than three assessments, then they receive a grade of "incomplete" and this grade becomes a failure within two weeks unless the work is completed in a satisfactory manner. This system meets the twin criteria of accuracy and helpfulness. It is accurate because it describes what the student can and cannot do. It focuses on proficiency, not the speed of achievement. It doesn't really make any difference whether the student achieved proficiency in the 1st week or the 8th week of the grading period; the objective of an effective grading system is that it accurately reflected student achievement when the grade was awarded. This system is helpful because students know precisely what they need to do in order to get a higher grade. Each assessment has a clear scoring guide (often called a "rubric") that describes student performance and sets forth the "rules of the game" for receiving higher scores. If you want a higher grade, you turn in work that meets the criteria for exemplary or proficient work. There is no mystery and little subjectivity.

This system actually saves teachers time. Contrast the "six assessment" system to the myriad of marks that dominate most grade books. We engage in Byzantine accounting drills that attempt to keep track of the debits and credits of homework, quizzes, extra credit, and all the other observations that compose the alchemy of grades. We should challenge the assumption that every observation by teachers must result in a mark in the grade book. In fact, the many assessments can be used for feedback and need not be used for evaluation.

Some people fear that students will not work hard unless every request by the teacher is associated with an entry into the grade book. This contention is not supported by evidence available in any school. Observe a music class or football practice. Our music educators routinely are able to conduct an orchestra rehearsal without once announcing that students who miss the F-sharp will receive a zero for that day in the grade book. The consequence of missing the F-sharp is obvious: They practice, practice, and practice some more until they master the F-sharp. Physical education classes and sports practices also routinely demonstrate how the feedback of coaches and teachers results in better performance, not an accounting drill in a grade book. It is a mystery to me why the concept of using assessment for feedback, rather than for evaluation, should be the exclusive province of music and physical education.

One final note about grading and standards: The average (or, more precisely, the arithmetic mean) has no place in a grading system that is accurate and helpful. Accuracy, after all, depends on the presumption that the grade is related to student achievement. The average, on the other hand, depends on the presumption that student performance during the first week of the quarter is equal in weight to a performance later in the quarter. Moreover, the use of the average presumes that all students in a class proceed on the journey to proficiency at the same pace. Parents and teachers know such an assumption to be unwarranted. When standards are used to determine a grade, the question is not when the student became proficient, but only that the student became proficient. Proficiency, not speed, is the criteria by which students are evaluated.

Q 39 Should students know how their assessments will be graded?

A Absolutely. Even in test formats that do not produce a scoring rubric, it is still an excellent strategy to use an "embedded rubric"; that is, place the elements of the rubric in the assessment item. For example, a writing or problem-solving prompt would include a sentence such as, "A complete response will include the following elements...." In this way, there is no mystery about what constitutes a proficient answer. The student has the responsibility for the thinking skills, but not the responsibility for guessing what format an evaluator requires to award a score of "proficient" on a test.

With regard to designing tests, my advice would be to engage in one of two strategies. Either provide the rubric used by the exam evaluators to teachers and students, or provide embedded rubrics in the writing prompt. By an "embedded rubric" I mean that the instructions in the text essentially repeat the requirements of the rubric. For example, let's consider a question in social studies about the causes of the French Revolution. Perhaps the teacher wrote the rubric so that a "proficient" response would include at least three supporting details, the identification of two important historical figures, and correct English conventions. In order to "embed" the requirements of this rubric in the writing prompt, the teacher would insert these words right after the test question:

"A complete response will include at least three supporting details and the identification of two important historical figures. For a response to receive a grade of proficient, it must be free of errors in grammar, spelling, and punctuation."

In this way, there is no ambiguity about the expectations of the teacher and the requirements of the student. No one can say, "You didn't tell me that!" or "I didn't know I had to do that!" or otherwise contend that teacher evaluation is a mystery.

Q 40 My district has assessments in place for each grade level in some content areas that reflect a 6-point rubric, but our report card uses a 4-point rubric to define overall performance levels. Can this still be effective and congruent in reporting progress, or should all rubrics be the same for each task that is assessed?

A First, let me congratulate you on the use of rubrics to communicate with students and parents about the quality of student work. This is far more constructive and clear than a series of letter grades that mean so many different things to different people.

With respect to consistency in rubrics, I prefer four-point rubrics. The fewer the points on the rubric, the more likely it is that teachers can find agreement on what a "3" or "proficient" really means. The more points on the rubric, the more individual variation in scoring. However, I also believe that consistency and clarity in communication is even more important. Thus when students find a "4" to be great in one context and only "adequate" in another context, they and their parents are understandably confused. Therefore, even though I'd prefer a four-point rubric, I would change to a six-point one if that was necessary to communicate with parents in a consistent manner. This is particularly true if you are taking information from assessments that have six points and then summarizing them in a "Standards Achievement Report." The summary should use the same terminology and measurements as the assessments that go into the summary.

With regard to the use of outside assessments, let me offer this advice. It is true that many assessments come with a four-point rubric: exemplary, proficient, progressing, and not meeting standards. If you change to a district-wide six-point rubric policy, then the assessment rubric can easily be adapted to this system. A score of 5-6 simply means "exemplary" in varying degrees; that is, work far beyond proficient-level work. A score of 4 means "proficient"; what you expect every regular education student to do. A score of 2-3 means "progressing"; the student understands what needs to be done to become proficient, but has not yet achieved that. A score of 1 is "not meeting standards"; the student needs intensive assistance and intervention in order to become proficient.

Q 41 When using a scoring guide, what is the best way to add the score to a grade book?

A The short answer is, "In pencil." The reason is that you want students to respect your feedback and use that feedback to improve their work. Their incentive for improvement is that you are not necessarily giving them their last grade—not the grade that is the result of their first effort. Remember, standards evaluate achievement, not time or pace of learning.

In addition, I do not recommend that you use a grade book with the traditional "one line per student." Rather, use a grade book that has a separate page for each student. In this way you can make a copy of that page at report card time, and both student and parents see the details supporting your grade. This helps give encouragement to the student with a low grade (at least they did some things well) and challenges the student with a higher grade (they need extra work in those areas).

Finally, let me recommend that the number of grades awarded in a period be small, such as six assessments during a 9-week grading period. For grading details, see the table on page 49.

42 When grading performance assessments, should we average the scoring guide results separately to derive a letter grade?

To develop a system of grading and reporting, two age-old practices must be abandoned. First, the practice of averaging student grades to determine a final grade is inappropriate and inaccurate. Second, assigning a score of "0" to a late or missing assignment does not accurately depict the students' learning. Couple a zero with grade averaging, and you have a deadly combination.

The average is not helpful and encourages fast, sloppy work. A better way is a small number of assessments with several opportunities to resubmit work. Rather than averaging the students' work, have them do it again until they score at least "proficient." If the work is "progressing" or "not meeting the standards," the student must resubmit the work. This is the objective and clear standard we have for everything from safety to immunization records to athletic contests: If they don't do it right the first time, they get another chance.

43 What data gathering techniques do you use, and when do you use them, when conducting performance assessment? Can you provide an example?

The most important data point a classroom teacher can gather is "percentage of students proficient or better" for each of the key standards. This is quite different from "average grade point" or "percentage correct" or "mean test score," which are the sort of statistics usually collected and used to represent student achievement. The focus on "percentage of students proficient or better" has two important implications. First, a fixed standard defines the educational objective. It doesn't matter whether the students score higher or lower than other classes and other schools; the only thing that matters is whether or not the students are proficient. This stops the false complacency that emerges when students and teachers claim, "We didn't meet the standard, but we're a lot better than the other schools." Second, the role of the teacher is not merely to render an evaluation and provide a good "spread" of student scores: some high, a lot in the middle, and some low. Rather, the responsibility of the teacher is to have as many students as possible achieve proficiency. This is the antithesis of the bell curve and the heart of standards-based instruction.

For an example, please refer to Appendix C, which contains an example of a standards-based report card.

Using Assessment Data to Improve Teaching and Learning

44 My school needs help using assessment data. We know that we have not been very effective at using the information we have gotten over the years to help us understand what we could be doing better, but we also feel that most of the information which we receive is not in small, diagnostic, useful pieces. Beyond this, we also notice that we are not able to help teachers become better consumers of this information. How can we improve?

There are two central issues. First, how do you use the information that you have? Second, what other information should you gather in order to use data constructively for the improvement of learning and teaching?

Although I share your frustrations with the data presentations provided by most state and national tests, there is some opportunity to gain valuable insights for curriculum and instructional leadership. First, identify the sub-scale differences. A general score on "reading" or "math" tells you very little, but the sub-scales can be quite revealing. Are the students stronger in fiction or in nonfiction? Are they stronger in measurement or in patterns and shapes? Are they better in calculation or problem solving?

By focusing your energy on sub-scales, you will accomplish several important things:

1. Initially, you will blunt the criticism that the analysis of scores "includes kids that I don't have, so it's irrelevant." In fact, if you find the same sub-scale difference in several different groups of students, that is evidence that the achievement difference is not an issue of a single group of students, but rather is a curriculum and instruction matter.

2. If two different groups of students display the same trends (stronger in fiction than nonfiction, for instance, or stronger in calculation than problem solving), then you know that teachers cannot simply excuse these differences by saying, "It's just the kids."

3. Moreover, by focusing on sub-scale strengths, you can ask teachers, "What did you do that made you so strong in this area?" That will lead to clues that can be transformed into strengths, such as more time, greater focus, and multi-subject integration. It's much easier for people to accept advice for change when the foundation of that advice came from their own successful practices.

The broader issue is that test scores alone don't tell us very much about how to improve student achievement. To use a medical analogy, it is the difference between an autopsy and a physical. An examination of test scores alone is the former: It tells us that the patient died, but gives scant clues as to why. A comprehensive accountability system includes not only test scores but also a systematic review of the "antecedents of excellence," which include measurement of effective practices in teaching, curriculum, assessment, and leadership.

Q **45** **We are currently researching and planning to implement an Assessment Data System that would automatically provide data to parents the same day of the assessment via e-mail, provide data to teachers on their students in the form of a simple graph, and provide data to administrators on a continual basis in the form of graphs. Are there special issues we should consider as we implement this assessment system?**

A Congratulations on your creation of a thoughtful and helpful system. Let me offer a couple of comments:

1. The automated e-mail to parents is excellent. I receive these now for some of my children and really appreciate it. It's especially helpful for parents who (like me) must travel a great deal.

2. There is a trade-off between speed and depth. I would recommend that you consider a balance between these same-day reports and other assessments that will, of necessity, be slower in reporting, but perhaps more valuable. The worst thing that could happen would be for a parent and student to feel "sucker-punched" by positive feedback on the daily tests, and then negative feedback on a more demanding essay or performance assessment later in the semester. Perhaps some caveat on each report would be appropriate, such as, "This is a partial report of progress and does not represent all the skills necessary for mastery of the standards in this class. For a more detailed report on your child's progress, please contact the teacher at any time."

3. The teacher graphs are a great idea. It would make us stop and say, "Wait a minute; 65% of my kids are not proficient in number operations. Should I really go on to the rhombus unit today, or should I adjust my schedule to meet the needs of my students?" Of course, I'm making a big leap here. Those graphs are only useful *if* teachers use them to change instruction. That is something I would certainly want to follow.

CHAPTER

4

Writing to Achieve

The Importance of Writing

46 My school wants to implement a journal writing time into our curriculum. I don't think journal writing will affect test scores. What is your opinion about journal writing?

Here's the bottom line on writing: Whether the writing happens in a journal, a Big Chief tablet, or on three-ring notebook paper isn't as important as *what happens to the writing* after the students have submitted it. The essence of successful writing includes:

1. Pre-writing
2. Rough Draft
3. Editing
4. Respect for teacher feedback and creation of final copy

It is perfectly acceptable for teachers to use journal writing as a method for steps 1 and 2, *as long as they continue* to steps 3 and 4. In other words, journal writing is fine, provided that both teachers and students follow through, reflect on what has been written, and work toward creating a final work product based on clear and effective feedback. If journal writing only consists of recording random thoughts without any purpose, context, feedback, editing, or revision, then it is very unlikely to help students improve their thinking, reasoning, reading, or writing skills. Indeed, I am seeing many journals used not for the purpose of building the love of written expression, but as an excuse for writing that is slovenly and scatological.

It comes down to this: If you want students to write better, you have to give them *feedback* and have them *practice* what you want them to do. That doesn't happen in typical journal writing that does not include teacher feedback and student re-writing.

You said that you don't believe that writing will affect test scores. That's a reasonable hypothesis that deserves to be tested. In fact, you probably already have the data to do so. You can examine the test results of classes in your district in which frequent writing assessment, along with systematic feedback and collaborative scoring, were predominant features of instructional practice. You can then compare those test results with classes where writing assessment was infrequent or completely absent. I have done this sort of comparison on a number of occasions and the results are clear: Frequent writing assessment is associated with higher test scores.

This association does not necessarily prove that writing "caused" higher scores, but only demonstrates that there is an association between writing and higher scores. Perhaps it is reasonable to consider this question: Even if writing had no impact on test scores, do my students need to improve their skills in written communication? Even if writing is irrelevant to my state accountability system, do I know that my students will receive a lifetime of benefits from improved writing skills? Whether or not you are correct in your skepticism about the relationship between writing and test scores, it may be that your students will nevertheless benefit from a greater emphasis on this vital skill.

47 Should things like grammar, spelling, and mechanics be included on rubrics for performance assessments?

Yes, spelling, grammar, and punctuation certainly do count. The more students write across disciplines, the higher their achievement and the higher their standardized test scores will be. Spelling, grammar, and other writing conventions should be part of scoring guides in subjects such as science, math, social studies, and art. Effective writing habits can only be developed with frequent writing and consistent scoring of mechanics in every subject.

You might consider separating mechanics from content using "two-rubric" grading. One rubric is focused on written expression while the other is devoted to academic content. For example, a lab report in science might have superior written expression and inadequate scientific reasoning, or deplorable expression with exemplary scientific analysis. Appendix D contains examples of two rubrics you might use in this instance.

48 We are having a controversy among the Language Arts teachers in our district as to the necessity of teaching cursive writing. Our state standards address "handwriting," not specifically cursive. We are aware of the urgency to teach content, style, etc. Is cursive writing an unnecessary skill in our technological age? What is the prevalent view among other educators? Early elementary teachers do not want to spend their time teaching cursive; however, high school teachers do not want to graduate a student who cannot write or read cursive. What is your opinion?

Many people would tell you that handwriting is an irrelevant skill. They would argue that with the advent of computers and, more particularly, software that translates the voice into the printed word, any sort of writing skill is rendered irrelevant. I respectfully dissent. My thesis in favor of writing generally and handwriting in particular is centered on the following arguments:

1. Writing is an extension of thinking. Research indicates that writing skills are highly related to other academic skills, including science, social studies, and mathematics. Contrary to popular belief, writing does not follow reading, but is an integral part of improving reading skills.

2. Writing is reflective. Teachers are overwhelmingly stressed because of the excessive demands on their time. A central cause of this stress is the preposterous notion that the teacher is the one and only "master evaluator" and the role of the student is limited to submitting work to the teacher. It is not only more efficient, but also far more educationally effective for students to read and reflect on their own work first before submitting it to the teacher. Of course, such reflection is only possible if the work of the student is legible. My advice that teachers require illegible work to be

re-submitted by students is not based on petulance and authoritarianism; it is rather based on the need for students to develop the critical thinking skill to read and reflect on their own work first.

3. Writing, and handwriting in particular, is communicative. Almost everyone holds dear a note from a student, child, or parent that was expressed with pen in hand. They have watched the light in a child's face when she received a "smiley face" with a handwritten "Great Job!" accompanying it. I want my students to be technologically literate, to use the Internet and e-mail. But I also want them to express thanks, longing, love, and a host of other emotions with their heart and pen. Their appreciation for this skill will come perhaps decades hence; certainly not within the nine months that I can guide them. As with so many other things I do in the classroom (once as a teacher, now as "helper dad"), I persevere not because it is popular but because it is right.

I do not make a brief for cursive over block letters. That argument is secondary to the central point that writing, and in particular legible handwriting, is essential for the intellectual development and helpful for the emotional development of our children. I want them to write letters, pen in hand, to parents, future spouses, and their children. As the recipient of handwritten letters from a father who could not see the ink on the page, I know that they will not regret the effort.

Teachers hesitate to demand legibility because students struggle to write. They fear that their demands might be "developmentally inappropriate." To those who would use this rationale to succumb to the temptation to demand high standards from their students, I would recommend the following: take a course in Chinese or Hebrew. I have done both. The humiliation of my inability to write well in these languages is tempered only by the fact that few people are willing to say that it is "developmentally inappropriate" for me to make Mandarin characters or an Aleph-vowel combination. My progress is slow, even painful (perhaps even more for my teachers than for me). But there are things I wish to say to students, teachers, friends, and family in Chinese and Hebrew that are not expressed adequately in English words or computerized typeface. The existence of computer programs that would ease the path by relieving me of the opportunity to write does not eliminate the value I gain from the attempt. I can only hope that the recipients of my letters (the same ones your students might send) of appreciation, recognition, and love will recognize not only the characters, but also the character within the missive.

I have perhaps made everyone in this controversy mad. Those who wish to maintain cursive as the only version of the King's English will be upset that I will accept block letters. Those who wish that I would say that handwriting is antiquated and irrelevant will be upset that I advocate legibility at all. At the very least, I hope that the length and seriousness of my response indicates my respect for all participants in this debate. I underestimate neither the value nor the difficulty of your profession. I offer not a prescription, but only the views of one parent and teacher, in that order.

Writing Across the Curriculum

49 I saw a speech in which Dr. Reeves presented some research on the correlation between persuasive writing and all other content areas. I would like to be able to cite that research. Could you please provide me with a reference or publication to go to for more information?

The relationship between writing and student achievement is not unique to my presentations, so let me offer several sources:

1. You can cite any of my public speeches, such as the one you attended. If you need a copy of the handouts, I'll be happy to send them to you. Just call us toll-free at 1.866.399.6019. You can also read articles on the subject at our web site: www.LeadandLearn.com.

2. *Educational Leadership*, February 2000, had a story of schools with the same relationship: more writing, higher scores (Noyce, Perda, & Traver).

3. Linda Darling-Hammond's excellent book, *The Right to Learn* (1997), has numerous citations of the relationship between increased performance assessment (an integral part of which is writing) and higher test scores.

There are two essential issues: First, there is abundant research to support more writing and more performance assessment. Second, even if I had no studies at all to support this contention, it should be clear to anyone who has reviewed student work in 99% of the schools in the country that the vast majority needs to write with better organization, accuracy, and expression. No studies are necessary to support that proposition. Just ask your colleagues: Are they satisfied with the quality of student writing? Do they believe that our current strategies to get quality student work are completely effective? Unless they can answer "yes" to both questions with certainty, you don't need any citations or studies. The kids need to write more.

50 How can we apply assessment writing to all content areas?

We need not render every math teacher a Hemingway. I have openly confessed my own literary ineptness. I'm a math teacher, and as with many of your colleagues, I might protest "I'm not an English teacher!" when you ask me to have students write across all content areas. If I think that "For Whom The Bell Tolls" is an AT&T advertising slogan and Dostoevsky is a really good hockey player, then please be patient with me. We can make writing assessment more accessible to every curriculum area if we consider the following ideas:

1. *Make it incremental*. Don't ask me to do "six trait" if I'm still struggling with simile, metaphor, and active voice. Let me focus on "two-trait" writing: organization and conventions. Every language arts teacher in the nation will be ecstatic if

colleagues in other disciplines focus on just those two traits, even if the rest of us non-Language Arts folks go to our grave simile- and metaphor-impaired.

2. *Let me cooperate with a colleague*. I don't want to tell my principal that I'm not a very good writer myself, and thus I'm hesitant to evaluate my students' lab reports or math explanations based on the content *and* the writing. So let me develop a collaborative assignment with a trusted language arts colleague in which students can earn credit in *both* of our classes, and we can share the grading duties.

3. *Make your demands reasonable*. Start with asking me to do a writing assessment once each quarter. That's not micro-management, it's clear, specific, and reasonable. When you say, "Do more writing across the curriculum," I don't know what you mean. When you say, "Please provide one writing assessment each quarter and let me know the percentage of students who were proficient; you can collaborate with other teachers and you need not evaluate all six traits of writing, just organization and mechanics," *then* it is clear what you are requiring of me and I retain a great deal of flexibility and freedom.

Writing to Improve

51 I recently found research showing that test scores improve when writing increases and improves. Do you have any similar research findings for higher education, specifically in medical and dental school?

A I'm not aware of research at the post-secondary level on the impact of writing on other areas of achievement. Certainly the accreditation agencies have placed an increased emphasis on integrative written activities to demonstrate student proficiency.

Whether or not I can support the notion that writing is synergistic with other disciplines, few people would say that they are satisfied with the level of student writing these days at any grade level, including college and university students. The experience of our colleagues in Massachusetts has been that when undergraduate writing samples are shown to the public, it is embarrassing for student and institution alike.

With regard to the issue of medical and dental students, their need to communicate more effectively both orally and in writing is demonstrated daily in courtrooms and in the offices of malpractice attorneys, not to mention their own examining rooms populated by bewildered patients. Educators who are preparing people for medical professions should not need to be convinced of the need for better communications and writing skills for their students.

None of this rhetoric responds to your request for evidence. Let me suggest a simple experiment. Ask a skeptical colleague to take just one section of students in one class that has traditionally been tested exclusively in a multiple-choice format. With that one section of one class, use a balanced approach: 50% performance assessment and 50% multiple choice. Then ask professors in the next class to evaluate student readiness for the *next* level of performance and compare their evaluations of students who had only multiple choice assessment to those with balanced assessment. The results of such a relatively simple, brief, and inexpensive experiment might be enlightening.

Q 52 **Our school is adding a computer-based curriculum to provide more reading and writing across the curriculum. Is there supporting data to prove that this kind of program is necessary and will work? We would also appreciate any research that you may have on any type of programs that will promote improvement in writing skills.**

A In order to help you more, I would need to know the specific computer program you are considering. I know that there is evidence to support LightSpan for the elementary grades, and good support for the "Write to Read" program cosponsored by IBM.

One problem with all computer-based programs is this: Kids don't take the tests using computers. They *must* learn to write clearly and effectively with pencil and paper. There simply is no substitute. Moreover, teachers, not computers, must give individual coaching and feedback to students. That doesn't mean computers have no place; it simply means they are nothing more than tools, not substitutes, for effective teaching. I've seen 1st - 6th graders totally enthralled with the LightSpan reading and math products. You might want to try them.

With regard to the best ways to improve writing scores, the best way by far is the use of a consistent writing scoring rubric and the very frequent use of student writing in multiple contexts: English, social studies, math, science, and other activities.

Effective Evaluation

53 I understand that it's important to evaluate all student writing with the same rubric. Can you give me an example of a writing rubric? How do I use it?

The use of the same rubric, or scoring guide, is important for the same reason that the use of the same rules of behavior is important: Students need consistency in order to learn what is expected of them. Good scoring guides use student-accessible language to identify precisely what "proficiency" means. Here are two different examples of scoring guides for persuasive writing:

Persuasive Writing Scoring Guide—Grades K-5

4 Exemplary

- ❍ Criteria in the Proficient category have been met.
- ❍ More advanced work is included. For example, the introduction grabs the reader's attention with vivid detail or different viewpoints on the topic. Other examples include: ________

3 Proficient

CONTENT

- ❍ The scope of the topic is appropriate for the length of the paper and is approved.
- ❍ Specific details are given in a way that keeps the readers attention. General, trivial statements are avoided.
- ❍ The sentences are original.

ORGANIZATION

- ❍ The introduction, body, and conclusion are included.
- ❍ Every topic sentence of the paragraph has supporting details.
- ❍ Every detail is in proper order.

LANGUAGE/WORD CHOICE

- ❍ The words are grade-level appropriate.
- ❍ Information is presented using metaphors, analogies, or any other device that personalizes the information.

SENTENCE STRUCTURE

- ❍ Complete sentences are used.
- ❍ A variety of sentences are used.
- ❍ Sentences begin in different ways.

MECHANICS

- ❍ There are no spelling, punctuation, capitalization, or grammatical errors in the final copy.

THE WRITING PROCESS

- ❍ The writing process was followed as directed in class, such as revise-edit.

2 Progressing

- ❍ Ten to twelve of the Proficient criteria are met.
- ❍ Revision and editing are required to meet the Proficient criteria.

1 Not meeting the standard(s)

- ❍ Fewer than ten of the Proficient criteria are met.

Persuasive Writing Scoring Guide—Grades 6-12:

4 Exemplary

- ❍ All of the characteristics for "proficient" plus the following:
- ❍ Enticing introduction, giving the reader an incentive to read the essay.
- ❍ Compelling evidence from multiple credible and qualified sources, using statistics and examples to make an overwhelming case in support of the arguments.
- ❍ Free of errors in grammar, spelling, and punctuation.

3 Proficient

- ❍ Opening paragraph begins with an introduction that clearly states the thesis and provides an overview of the essay.
- ❍ Each subsequent paragraph begins with a topic sentence.
- ❍ Thesis is supported by evidence, including statistics or examples from published sources, with appropriate citation.
- ❍ Only slight errors in grammar, spelling, or punctuation. None of the errors prevents the reader from understanding the meaning of the text.
- ❍ If project is done on a word processor, style requirements are followed. If project is completed by hand, the writing is legible.

2 Progressing

- ❍ The paragraphs are related to the topic, but do not clearly support the thesis.
- ❍ The evidence is not related to the claim made in the text or the citations are incomplete.
- ❍ Errors in grammar, spelling, or punctuation detract from a clear understanding of the text.
- ❍ Word processing format does not follow style requirements. Handwriting is not legible.

1 Not meeting the standard(s)

- ❍ The paragraphs are not related to the topic. The thesis is not supported.
- ❍ There is no evidence and there are no citations.
- ❍ Errors in grammar, spelling, or punctuation detract from a clear understanding of the text.
- ❍ Word processing format does not follow style requirements. Handwriting is not legible.
- ❍ The assignment needs to be re-done.

54 How can I share writing samples and practice external scoring with my fellow teachers?

Let's start with something very simple. At one faculty meeting, department meeting, or grade level meeting, take a single piece of student work (please remove the name of the student and the identification of the school). Staple a scoring guide to the front of it. Duplicate this and ask people to score it and see if you can reach a consensus. This doesn't have to be a daylong staff development exercise. It can be a 20-minute part of a meeting. You are trying to build a culture of collaboration, and it will take a lot of continuous work and reinforcement. Eventually, you can have exemplary work on the walls, in the trophy case, and as an integral part of every parent conference, staff development meeting, and leadership discussion.

CHAPTER

5

Standards and Electives

55 In my observations of high-achieving schools, I have noted several common characteristics such as collaboration, a focus on standards, and multiple assessment measures. However, another surprising similarity emerged: Many also focus on the arts. What is the role of the arts in schools today? How do you make it vital to achievement in language arts and math? What is the research in this area?

Your observation that high achievement is consistent with a focus on the arts is right on the mark. I'm finding that many people honor multiple intelligences in abstract conversation, but not in action. In fact, however, music, drama, and art are all not only personally enriching, but integral to the academic achievement of students. I recently conducted a review of the goals established by more than 160 schools. One might think that those schools that exclusively emphasized academic pursuits would have had the highest scores. In fact, even after controlling for demographic factors, those schools with the highest academic results had chosen to make one of the top five areas of emphasis the performing and visual arts, extracurricular activities, and community service. The path to academic achievement is not rendering school a joyless boot camp, but the active integration of the arts and extracurricular activities into the life of every student.

Rather than engage in the typical argument about whether the arts are "academic" or should "stand alone," I prefer to view all subjects as inherently integrated. Asking teachers to integrate writing and mathematics into science is hardly novel; the same is true of measurement in physical education, fractions in music, or geometry in art. The more context and integration we can provide to students, the better they are.

There is abundant research on this, and I'm not talking about the fairly specious arguments of *The Mozart Effect* (Campbell, 1997). Far more sound research has been done by David Perkins and Howard Gardner, co-directors of Project Zero at Harvard. In particular, see Perkins' splendid book, *Outsmarting IQ* (1995), and Gardner's difficult but worthwhile text, *The Disciplined Mind* (1999).

56 Do you know of any school district that has had the courage to dump some or all of its electives that were not supporting the academic standards? If they have done so, how are they doing now?

I can think of two that have. Both of them moved 9th and 10th grade students who do not meet reading and math standards into double math and double literacy courses, and yes, that pushes out other classes that do not contribute to meeting standards. They are rewarded with better student achievement. Note well, however, that this does not destroy elective courses. Rather, it creates a reasoned priority: Students must read and succeed academically in order to survive in high school and in life. Rather than eliminate elective courses, schools could defer a social studies or science course, requiring the 9th graders who need it to take an extra hour of literacy, and then take the 9th grade social studies course in the 10th grade. It is true that in the final two years of high school, these students might have fewer electives, more courses, or some combination of those alternatives. It is also true that they will be much more successful in high school and beyond as a result of the thoughtful choices made early in their secondary school education. This adds only some minor inconvenience to the schedule and offers the great benefit of having students able to read the social studies and science textbooks.

I am always challenged by the statement that the establishment of academic priorities "won't work" or "can't be accepted" or "isn't consistent with school culture." Wait a minute: If a student came to school and didn't meet the vaccination standards, would we have so much angst about it, or would we just get the student the vaccination? If a student didn't meet the standards for playing on an athletic team, perhaps because she had not yet received the proper medical documentation, would we look the other way or insist that the standard be met? That's the issue on matters we really care about, such as vaccinations, safety, football, and basketball: We get the student what they need, when they need it, because we all believe that, for matters of health, it's necessary and obvious to make such priorities. Only on things less important, such as reading, mathematics, and writing, do we worry that the remedy might be inconvenient. Pardon the cynicism, but the reality is this: We know what to do, and we must decide, as a community and as educators, if we have the will to do it. If we don't, then we cannot blame the kids and their parents.

57 Should art be utilized as an area unto itself, or must it be incorporated into other areas such as reading, social studies, or math? Can elementary students be expected to participate in art during the school day?

There need not be a dichotomy between "academic art" and "just plain art." Students can do wonderfully creative artistic projects and also reinforce academic areas that are essential for all students. Examples include:

1. Creative projects linked to vocabulary words. Many students are visual learners, and the use of artistic images to reinforce vocabulary terms is a wonderful intersection of language arts and visual art.

2. Perspective in art. An essential artistic skill, perspective, also enhances student understanding of scale, ratio, and geometric principles.

3. Geometric shapes in art. I have seen terrific student artwork that is entirely based on different colors and sizes of triangles. This allows creative imagination to soar while reinforcing some core geometric and measurement concepts.

4. Story boards in social studies. Students need to understand time lines and the meaning of historical events, and visual images can make the text come alive.

5. Set designs for plays in literature or social studies.

The list goes on and on. It is unnecessary and destructive to say that "pure" art excludes academic subjects. Art is rich, inventive, and creative. It will reach many students who are unsuccessful in other classes. Rather than be an "escape" from academics, students can use art (and music, physical education, etc.) to make critical connections to academic subjects, and still have a great time doing it.

Q 58 How can we justify continuing to have computer lab, library, music, and physical education in the instructional day?

A We justify the continuation of these programs because, if implemented properly, they make vital and important contributions to student learning. You might consider adapting these subjects to a "block" system in which you offer them for fewer periods during the day, each of which are longer in duration. This allows the physical education and music teachers much better opportunities to accomplish their objectives, and far less time is spent setting up, breaking down, lining up, moving around, and getting organized. It is also important to include specific academic content in each of these areas. In computer lab, students can write essays and stories. In physical education class, students can keep mathematically correct charts, graphs, and tables of their performance. In art class, students can master geometric shapes, scale, ratio, and proportion. In the library, students can write, research, and write some more. In other words, *every* program and class is directly supportive of academic standards. Many highly effective coaches, music teachers, and media center specialists are doing this right now.

Q 59 I'd love to see my kids playing on the community soccer team and taking violin lessons, but the schools seem to think they should do nothing but study for the spring achievement test. Do you think extracurricular activities are detrimental to a child's studies? Will they be too tired or too distracted to concentrate in school?

I strongly endorse your commitment to music, athletics, and other extracurricular activities. Although it is true that a few students are absurdly overloaded with activities that fill every waking moment of their day, your question implies that you seek a reasonable balance. Playing on a soccer team and taking a music lesson every week certainly does not interfere with student achievement. In fact, there is substantial evidence that participation in extracurricular activities contributes to student achievement both in terms of grades and on state achievement tests. Two recent studies from a national sample of 25,000 high school students, for example, noted that participation in athletics was associated with positive attitudes toward school and improved student behavior (Viadero, 1999).

Even if there were not abundant evidence about the value of extracurricular activities, there are common sense reasons to maintain most of these vital programs. Ask any secondary educator to name the essential knowledge and skills for success in their class. They invariably list not only academic content knowledge, but also such personal skills as teamwork, persistence, organization, time management, and work ethic. These are characteristics that are likely to be acquired in music, athletics, student council, drama, debate, and a host of other extracurricular activities.

Perhaps the backlash against some extracurricular activities has occurred because, in a few instances, school sports have dominated athletics and in some other instances, parents have traumatized children with excessive involvement in non-school activities. These few exceptions, however, do not diminish the overall positive impact of extracurricular activities of the social and academic life of children.

CHAPTER

6

Student Motivation

60 Motivation of students within our district is a problem. What about those who refuse to try or complete any work?

It is possible that a student is motivated by absolutely nothing and refuses any adult instruction. Such a student should be evaluated for profound emotional disturbance and referred to the appropriate special education professional.

However, this question most likely refers to many regular kids who simply aren't very engaged in school. The same kids, however, *do* find some things highly motivating. I've seen very effective teachers tap into that motivation, often in cooperation with their colleagues in music, art, and physical education. They find the one or two areas that the student finds interesting and engaging, and use those as incentives and connections to academic subjects. After all of these attempts, however, you have a policy to enforce. If a student refuses to comply with school policy, he or she must face the consequences. Perhaps it means a change in curriculum or, in the most severe cases, a move to an alternative school. The critical issue is this: We need not wait until a student has failed or dropped out of school to make essential intervention decisions. Most teachers know which students are at risk for failure and what course of action should be taken in October. Waiting until the next spring or summer to take such decisive action is wasteful in time, money, and emotion for both the teachers and the students.

61 I have about six students who consistently make D's and F's or do not turn in assignments at all. I have tried having students with missed work or work below 70% re-do and make up work. All of this takes hours of extra time each week. Then I found most did not improve. What do we do in situations like this when we have a large number of students who are not achieving and are not willing to even try?

You have addressed a very important subject: student motivation. You are entirely right to be concerned that the awarding of low grades has little or no effect on these students. Our observation is that many students may not respond to poor grades. In fact, low grades have the opposite impact: A "D" is really a reward for bad work. It tells the student that their failure to meet your standard did not result in any meaningful consequence and that their failure (what a "D" really means) will simply be someone else's problem next year. A better idea is that, when confronted with unacceptable work, the teacher consistently and immediately enforces high standards. In this scenario, the teacher does not wait for papers to be turned in again several weeks after a poor performance. Rather, at the very moment that the paper is returned by the teacher the first time with comments on it, the class stops, and the teacher's feedback results in revision and resubmission. Not the next week; not the next day; immediately. This practice can be somewhat inconvenient and disruptive at first, but it makes the powerful point that your feedback deserves respect and that the students must respond to your feedback instantly.

62 Why is it that some students just aren't motivated? Is it the parents? A lack of self-esteem? I feel that knowing the source of my students' apathy might help me combat it.

The honest answer is, "I don't know." This perplexes me as a parent (at this writing, kids in elementary, middle, and high school) and as a teacher. A student can be engaged and interested one day, and utterly bored and disinterested the next. One day homework is timely and accurate and the next day it is missing in action. One project elicits interest and the next receives only an apathetic reaction. We tend to one of two extremes when faced with unmotivated students. One extreme is to dismiss them with the callous statement, "They're here to learn, I'm here to teach, and if they don't like it, tough." I've witnessed many teachers throw in the towel on promising students who, for the moment, are unmotivated, and I understand, but disagree with, the frustration and anger of those teachers. The other extreme, however, also is doomed to failure. The teacher who begs, cajoles, and pleads for student involvement and then rewards inadequate work is also traveling a perilous path in which we risk not only the unmotivated student, but the motivated students who wonder why their work fails to elicit such effort by the teacher.

What's the reasonable middle ground? Let me offer these ideas to promote (but certainly not guarantee) student motivation.

1. *Offer choice*. We can offer far more choice than we do, including choices of projects, topics, test items, and even homework assignments. To many students, and particularly to adolescents, choice is equated with freedom, and freedom is exceedingly motivating. Choice certainly does not diminish academic rigor. In fact, I have seen exceptionally demanding secondary school teachers produce a list of 25 essay questions that will be on an exam and indicate that students will have a choice to write on any five of them. This practice completely removes any element of surprise and thus removes excuses for the failure of students to be prepared. This encourages depth of preparation rather than superficial memorization of many different unrelated things. Most importantly, students have the opportunity to find something in which they are genuinely interested. I might add that, from a psychometric point of view, assessment is more accurate when students have a choice of items because the teacher must focus on the ability of the student to respond to the item and the clarity of the student's expression. It makes it impossible to compare one student's work to that of another student, which is the antithesis of grading.

2. *Encourage student participation* in the creation of learning contracts, assignments, scoring guides (rubrics), and examinations. Students have a fundamental understanding of fairness, and there are few times in their student lives that they are able to influence, not to mention create, the rules of the game. Students are, by the way, invariably more rigorous in their expectations of themselves and their colleagues than their teachers and parents tend to be.

3. *Create "menus" of assignments*. If one particular assignment is not motivating—perhaps for home and personal reasons completely beyond the control of the teacher—then allow the student to thoughtfully choose to punt it. We must pick our battles carefully, and universal completion of every blank in the grade book is not nearly as essential as careful work and maximum engagement in seven out of ten assignments.

4. *Take some time to observe* what the student does find motivating. A brilliant high school English teacher told me of her experience in trying to reach a student who appeared headed for failure. She followed him to basketball practice every afternoon for a week and sat in the bleachers. She observed the high-fives, the reprimands, the clarity of expectations, the unambiguous definition of success, and the immediate gratification of superb performance. While the basketball coach and literature teacher had not been professionally close prior to that time, she confessed that she learned a lot about teaching English from the coach. She started providing immediate feedback to her students, sometimes within moments. She found that many students, including the troubled young man on the basketball team, assumed that one either "had it" or "didn't have it" in English, and that success was a matter of inborn skill. The rules of grammar, expression, and literary analysis that the teacher thought were clear were, in fact, a mystery. She took a great deal of class time to define, in language accessible to all students, what "success" meant in English class. She created models of improvement, following an essay through several revisions. This was, she opined, the literary equivalent of "game films" in which the basketball students would systematically analyze errors and discuss how to improve their performance in the future. Did this transform the unmotivated student into Hemingway? Probably not. But it certainly made it clear that both teacher and student could learn from one another, and the teacher took an enormous first step by observing a context in which the student was motivated. Almost every student is motivated in some context, be it music, dance, athletics, creative expression, or martial arts. If we can find that

context and adapt it to the classroom, we have a much better opportunity to motivate students. For more on this subject, see Rogers, Ludington, and Graham's excellent book, *Motivation and Learning: A Teacher's Guide to Building Excitement for Learning and Igniting the Drive for Quality* (1998).

63 I'm worried about posting samples of "exemplary" student work. Will it be the same kids over and over who have their work displayed?

It is not necessary to use *this* year's students for the exemplary work. In fact, it is most useful to display work of an anonymous student. Remember, the purpose of displaying exemplary work is not recognition of one student, but rather the building of evaluative skills by all students. Students can compare their work to the "target work" and ask, "Do I have my name on my paper, my paragraphs indented, and my sentences beginning with a capital letter?" Whether the "target" is a descriptive paragraph in the 3rd grade or a 25-page term paper for a high school student, models are exceptionally valuable for students and teachers.

The teacher can accurately say, "This is the work of a student who was just like you. She had a hard time at first, but she worked and worked and worked, and just look at what she was able to do!" In other words, make it clear that the "exemplary" product is not the result of spontaneous effort by the child, but the result of thinking about the teacher's feedback, comparing work to the objective, and trying again.

The source of real self-esteem is letting children know that they are not merely the sum of their self-estimations when they walk into the classroom door. Instead, students are wonderfully capable people who can do terrific things, if only they try, try, and try again, and keep listening to the teacher's feedback.

64 How do we show parents exemplary work without showing them someone else's paper?

A: You need not give them the name of the student on the exemplary paper. It is very helpful for parents to see what a "real" student of the same age and ability as their own child can do. The variable is not "higher IQ" or "more innate ability." It is typically better organization, harder work, and more respect for the teacher's feedback. Parents who would never read a rubric on a scoring guide for an assessment will be able to look at the performance of their own children, and then compare it to other children of the same age and background. No names need be disclosed, but it's essential that parents and students and teachers have models of what good performance looks like. I encourage teachers to save examples of work at the end of each year so that they can begin the year not with an abstract notion of good student performance, but rather with concrete examples of what students will achieve by the spring.

CHAPTER

7

Interventions for Under-performing Students

Intervening for Student Success

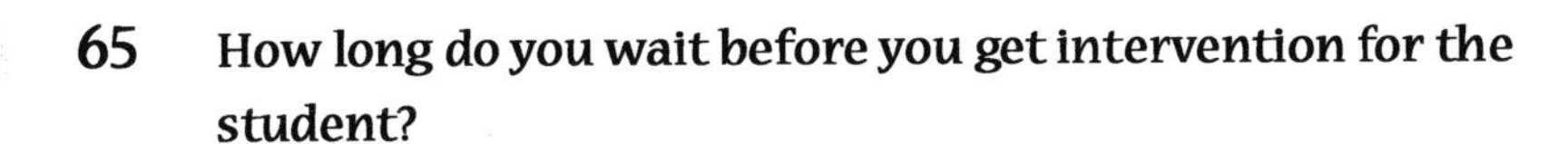

65 How long do you wait before you get intervention for the student?

Retention almost never works as a device to improve student achievement. In fact, it usually has the opposite result. A better alternative is *immediate* and decisive intervention. If a child comes to 4th grade unable to read, we need not wait until the end of that academic year to make a retention/promotion decision. We need to intervene *now*, with a restricted curriculum and a highly controlled set of expectations. This also, of course, requires very clear communication with the parents. Interventions can include time before and after school.

66 Which programs have been most successful to deal with underperforming students at the high school level?

There are two consistent keys to improved achievement in secondary schools: more writing, particularly informative writing in multidisciplinary contexts, and more collaboration, particularly when teachers jointly evaluate real student work and forge a consensus about what constitutes "proficiency" in their schools. Finally, the consistent practice in successful secondary schools is their willingness to intervene quickly and decisively. If a 9th grader cannot read the social studies textbook, do we really need to wait until the end of the spring semester and multiple failures to recognize that the student needs assistance? There are a growing number of schools where students receive double English and double math as 9th and 10th graders if this is what they need to succeed. They do not wait for failure at the end of the 9th grade. Instead, they intervene early. Of course, this means that there are some really upset 15-year-olds who discover that they don't get to pick their own courses anymore. Sometimes the opportunity to regain choice helps to motivate them to better performance. In another district, a five-year follow-up study of students who received mandatory intervention in grade 9 found that these students had higher grades, lower dropouts, and higher levels of participation in post-secondary education than students who did not receive this intervention. Notice that the remedy was not to have 18-year-old 8th graders; the successful remedy was intervention and curriculum control. The entire issue of the December 2000 Bulletin of the National Association of Secondary School Principals is devoted to this matter, and I have an extensive article in it, entitled "Essential Transformations for the Secondary School," that elaborates on my ideas for the important changes necessary for high schools.

Fighting the Retention Temptation

67 What do we do with children who make gains throughout the year, but don't meet the standards that are set in that grade level? We have so many children who come to us below grade level. Is retention really fair for those children? Can't we measure their *growth* instead of measuring whether they met the standards?

This is a policy matter to be addressed by your school, but let me offer a few suggestions for you to consider. In general, it is a great idea to measure "growth" as you suggest, but growth is not a substitute for meeting standards. Students must have both growth and academic achievement that meets the state requirements. So what do you do with students who, as you suggested, demonstrate growth, but do not meet the standards? If we fail to prepare these students for the next grade level, then the problem is simply magnified in future years. Consider the chart in Figure 7.1, based on an analysis of more than 6,000 pieces of student work. It clearly shows that as students progressed, less and less was expected of them because a lower percentage of the work done by these students was on grade level. The teachers in this school might have argued, "But they were showing progress!" Nevertheless, when 5th graders are only asked to do 2% of their work at the 5th grade level, they are being set up for failure in middle school.

Figure 7.1 — Mathematics Grade-Level Gap
Source: *DataWorks Newsletter*, February 2000, p. 1

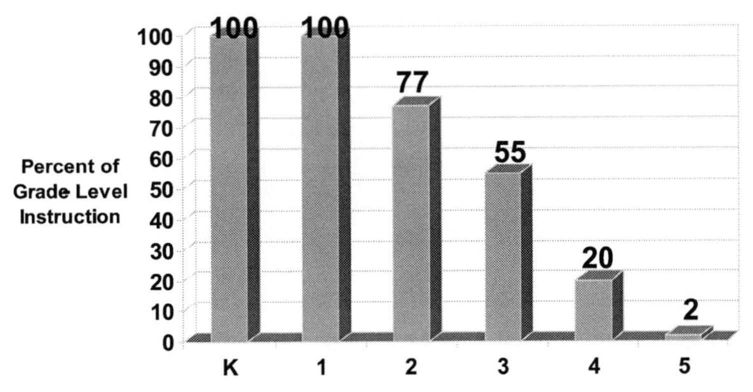

Figure 7.2 Language Arts Grade Level Gap
Source: *DataWorks Newsletter*, February 2000, p. 1

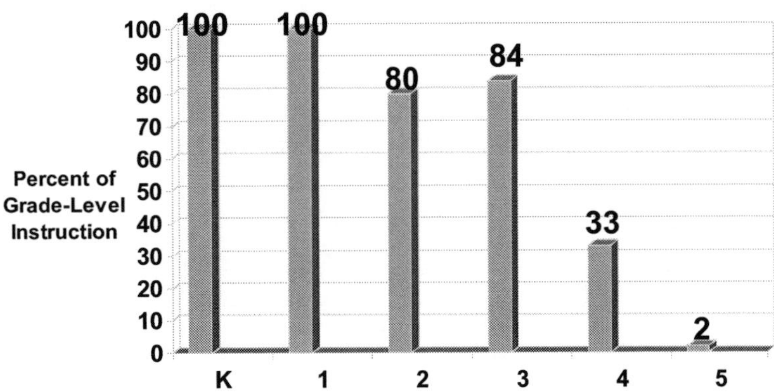

Because lowered standards and expectations are not adequate solutions, here are some practical ideas that you might wish to consider:

1. *Multi-age classroom*. The situation you have described might suggest the use of a multi-age classroom. There will always be children who come to you below grade level. Rather than force you into a promotion or retention decision at the end of each year, the multi-age classrooms allow for a continuum of grades (typically two or three grade levels at a time) so that you can get children up to speed in reading and writing first, then concentrate on other subjects.

2. *Looping*. If multi-age classrooms are not a possibility in your school, another alternative is "looping," in which the same teacher has the responsibility for the same group of children for several years in a row. This means that the teacher is not typecast as a "First Grade Teacher" exclusively, but rather takes responsibility for the full spectrum of learning from Kindergarten through third grade, and stays with the children for four consecutive years. If there is a problem with a child, that problem is not "passed on" to someone else, but the same teacher retains responsibility for getting all children to the appropriate grade level by the end of the final year of the loop.

3. *Intervention programs*. Another alternative is intensive intervention programs, including extra hours for reading, writing, and mathematics during the school day, after hours, or during the summer. I am working with schools that routinely offer 2-3 hours of reading every day for all students, with an additional 1-2 hours for students who are not reading on grade level. These schools have an all-out commitment that every teacher in every class is a reading teacher, and that above all, reading skills are necessary for future student success.

The ultimate answer to your question, however, is that we cannot accurately say that "getting better" is a substitute for academic achievement. When we engage in that practice, we are only creating a group of students who face extreme frustration and failure in later grades. When the elementary teachers say, "These challenges are not developmentally appropriate, and the children can get it later," and the middle school teachers say the same thing, we are left with a group of 9th and 10th grade students who cannot read, write, or compute. The plain fact is that students must have high expectations from an early age, and the most important and respectful thing our teachers can do is to insist upon those high expectations early. We cannot accept the proposition that kids "can't do it" if they are cognitively able to meet our requirements.

68 With all the emphasis on accountability and test scores, what is the current wisdom on retaining children in their current grade if they are not performing at "grade level"? There is research out there that supports both sides of the question.

The research on the subject is ambiguous. The prevailing wisdom had been that retention of students greatly magnifies the likelihood of future problems, including dropping out of high school. More recent research has suggested some instances in which retention is not so destructive. You can find studies on both sides of the subject at www.edweek.org, searching for the terms "retention and promotion." That said, I have yet to meet the 5th grade teacher who is enthusiastic about having 14-year-old students in class, or the 7th grade teacher who welcomes 18-year-olds.

The most successful programs we have observed for students not meeting standards is neither retention nor social promotion, but intensive intervention. For students not reading on grade level, they *get more time* in literacy. In practice, this means that some students get up to three hours a day of literacy if that is what they need. Hoping that they will just "get it" with enough repetition at the rate of one hour per day is folly. Interestingly, this does not mean that these students lose all their electives and special courses. It does mean that if you have 9th grade students reading at a 6th grade reading level, their time must be focused on literacy, and the 9th grade biology and history courses (with textbooks that the student cannot read) wait until 10th grade. Sometimes that means a 2-hour block the next year, or simply pushing the 9, 10, 11 block of social studies and science to a 10, 11, 12 block. In any case, we stop the bizarre notion that "doing algebra louder" or "doing English faster" is the solution to students who are below grade level.

69 What do we do about the student with a lower I.Q. that continues to be retained for not making grade level? What do we do about self-esteem problems that may arise because of this?

If a student qualifies for special education, then the provisions of the Individualized Education Plan govern them. If, however, the reference to "lower I.Q." means that the students are simply processing information in a different way or at a slower pace, but they are indeed capable of meeting the standard, then repeating a grade doesn't make any sense, and neither does social promotion. These students need more focus and time on core academic skills, and they can get it during the regular school day. This implies that some choices might need to be made if these students need an extra hour of writing or an extra 40 minutes of math.

Advantages of the Multiple Intelligences Classroom

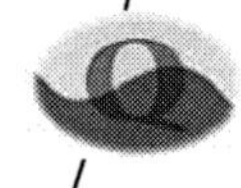

70 How can we address the total child?

One of the most important issues to consider is the emotional needs and multiple intelligences of the children we serve. We address the former through multiple opportunities to learn. We reject the notion that all students acquire and process information at the same rate and in the same way. Encouragement, not just evaluation, is the result. This means that some assessments are diagnostic: They are conducted to understand what the student knows, and not merely to enter a grade in a grade book. We address the multiple intelligences issue through the deliberate and specific use of music, art, physical education, and other opportunities to help the student make connections. Howard Gardner (1999) writes passionately about this in *The Disciplined Mind*: We don't use multiple intelligences to create alternatives (music rather than math), but rather to create connections. In Professor Gardner's own words:

> A belief in multiple intelligences, however, is in no sense a statement about standards, rigor, or expectations, and it is certainly not a rejection of these desiderata. On the contrary: I am a demon for high standards and demanding expectations. I do not always succeed in my own life and work, but it is not for lack of trying. It pains me to see my work aligned (I could have written "maligned") with that of individuals who are apologists for low standards, low expectations, "anything goes."
>
> Perhaps there is little that I can do to correct such a misrepresentation. But I can state, as emphatically as I know how, that an education for all human beings is an education that demands much for all of us — teachers as well as students, societies as well as individuals, and (if I may) readers as well as writers. Moreover, an education for all human beings cannot succeed unless we have ways of ascertaining what has been understood and what has been mildly or fatally misconstrued. I envision a world citizenry that is highly literate, disciplined, capable of thinking critically and creatively, knowledgeable about a range of cultures, able to participate actively in discussions about new discoveries and choices, willing to take risks for what it believes in. (p. 25)

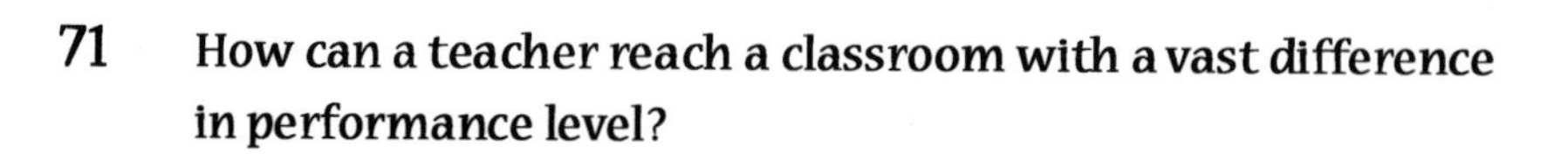

71 How can a teacher reach a classroom with a vast difference in performance level?

The most important key is to reduce "whole group" instruction by a significant amount. The teacher is a coach and guide, so lecturing to the entire group with the vast differences described in this question does not make sense. Assessments, projects, and assignments should have a spectrum of tasks, from basic through enrichment. We expect every student to accomplish mastery of the basic requirements, but we do not expect them all to accomplish this at the same rate, pace, and time. Coaching, rather than lecturing, also liberates the teacher to spend more time with students who need help on the fundamentals without subjecting the entire class to a review of material that is already mastered. This technique also permits the teacher to devote time to students who need enrichment without bewildering others in the class who are not prepared for that instruction.

72 I recently heard you speak briefly on looping. I was hoping you might be able to elaborate on your views about looping and/or give me any additional information sites. I would greatly appreciate your help.

First, let me confess my personal prejudice in favor of looping because of my daughter's exceptionally successful experience with a gifted teacher in a grade 4-5 loop. It has not only been successful for Julia, but for many other students of widely varying ability and academic backgrounds.

That said, let me replace my parent hat with my researcher's hat. It is probably not looping itself that is the variable here, any more than block scheduling is a variable in secondary school. In fact, these things are tools that require educators to use effective practices. For example, if I am teaching in a looping situation, what does that imply?

1. I must construct detailed plans for an extended curriculum, putting the pieces of the puzzle together over more than then a single year. Coverage gives way to learning.

2. I must accept the reality that my students proceed at different rates, paces, and times. Speed is no longer the variable, but learning is the imperative. That means that I have assessments that include multiple tasks. I know that my students are not clones—that some need challenge while others need foundation—so I never use a single-task assessment. This implies...

3. ...that the amount of whole-group instruction that I use has diminished to almost nothing. It is little more than the pledge and morning greeting, and I'm not too sure about those things! After that, it's chaos (the good kind of chaos, that is). This chaos reflects a nonlinear, non-predictable system, and is an accurate reflection of my classroom.

In sum, it is not "looping" as a policy, but rather the professional practices that result from looping that make it effective. By analogy, it is not block scheduling itself at the secondary level, but the professional practices, such as better assessment, more differentiated instruction, and improved curriculum focus, that cause improvements in student achievement. Looping (or any other reform) without changes in professional practice is impotent. It's as bad, to conclude the analogy, as saying that with block scheduling, the only impact is that "now I can show the whole movie instead of splitting it up over two days."

73 If I am measuring student achievement rather than time, how does that affect the fact that I operate on a strict 9-month calendar? Allowing multiple 'do-overs' is a wonderful concept, in theory. But how can I manage multiple do-overs and still have the class ready for promotion at the end of nine months?

Excellent point. If we really want to recognize that students acquire and process information at different rates, what does that imply for our time schedules? There are three things to consider:

1. "Multiple opportunities" for submitting work should not be "infinite opportunities" for submitting work. A reasonable middle ground might be 1-2 weeks for re-submission at the secondary level and 1-2 days at the elementary level. Teacher feedback and coaching is never respected in a "one shot" assessment. Students will simply discard the feedback, knowing it is futile even to read it. When teacher feedback is used to improve student performance, however, the re-submission of work gives teachers more respect and improves student performance. In fact, it can also save time because the standards for submission of work are clearer and less time is spent writing the same comment on 28 papers.

2. There will be students who require an extra hour of math and literacy every day. There is no justification for saying we "don't have the time" to give them that extra hour, when having that student repeat a grade or a course would take at least as much time. It is simply unfair for principals and teachers to have students waste nine months in classes while they wait for the final judgment when instead there could be early and decisive intervention in their academic career. These interventions can be inconvenient and difficult, but not nearly as much so as having the student repeat a grade.

3. When it comes to saving time, principals can be of immense help by "weeding the garden"; that is, identifying the activities, chapters, and projects that waste time. They can eliminate these time wasters, or coach teachers to change the nature of time robbers into more constructive academic activities. Some time-wasting weeds are self-imposed (such as elaborate bulletin boards constructed by teachers) and others are traditional (such as innumerable holiday celebrations without academic connections). In light

of this, we must challenge the notion that there is "no time" for improved assessment and student coaching when, in fact, a great deal of time is within the teachers' discretion and at least a few of those hours involve activities that should be discontinued.

74 Do you have research that shows whether 4th grade students learn better in one classroom with one teacher teaching all the subjects or in multiple classrooms with a different teacher for each subject?

The short answer is, "No." I am not aware of definitive research with classic experimental and control groups on this subject. There is, however, a substantial body of qualitative research, case studies, and common sense on the matter. An increasing number of states have high-stakes tests at the 4th and 5th grade levels and have, at the same time, adopted rigorous and content-laden standards in the core academic subjects for 4th and 5th grade. A cursory reading of the math and science expectations for many 4th and 5th grade students makes clear that a large number of people with an elementary teaching certificate do not have the background or interest to address some of those standards. This is not their fault. It is a misalignment between the demands of undergraduate teaching curricula and the demands of academic standards for math and science in upper elementary schools. What's the answer? Not necessarily to make 4th and 5th grade into mini-middle schools, but certainly there are abundant examples of two teachers sharing classes (typically switching at lunch), with one teacher emphasizing language arts and social studies, and the other emphasizing math and science.

Back to your original question on the research: What abundant research (Darling-Hammond, 1997; Wong, 1999; Haycock, 1998; Marzano & Kendall, 1996; and even Reeves, 2000) makes clear is that teacher quality is the most dominant variable in student performance, far greater than any demographic characteristic. As a result, we must invest in teacher quality, and an important part of that is not only pedagogical

knowledge, but content knowledge. In the meantime, good intentions are not a substitute for understanding the subject matter being taught, and thus some team teaching just makes common sense.

CHAPTER

8

Accountability

The Basics of Accountability

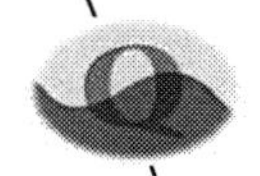

75 What exactly is an accountability system? Reading the newspapers makes me think that accountability is something that serves as punishment for teachers and schools who don't do their jobs. My kids' teachers hate the idea that they are going to be accountable for what kids do (or fail to do) on state tests. But every politician and school board member around here seems to think accountability is a great idea. Who's right?

Your question reflects the image that is quite common today: teachers loathe accountability while political leaders love it. In fact, many teachers I know would embrace educational accountability if it were fair, meaningful, and comprehensive.

Let's start with the fundamental purpose of educational accountability. Why, after all, should people in any endeavor be accountable? Some people might suggest, as your question does, that the primary purpose of accountability is punishment. If that were the case, we would only be able to use school accountability systems after students have failed. That's somewhat like saying that the only purpose of laws in a society is to lock people up, rather than to prevent crime. Is the only purpose of the health requirements in schools for the vaccination of students and cleanliness in the school cafeteria to expel unvaccinated kids and reprimand cafeteria employees? Or, is the purpose of those requirements to make our schools a safe and healthy place in which to learn? Just as the primary purpose of health regulations is to preserve the health and safety of our children, the primary purpose of educational accountability is the improvement of student learning. Once we understand this primary purpose, we can get to the heart of your question: What is an accountability system?

A meaningful system of educational accountability should have three key components:

1. It should have information about student achievement. Although we all know the limitations of standardized tests, they do provide at least a snapshot (though certainly not a comprehensive review) of student achievement. Just as blood pressure readings are not a complete physical, test scores are not a complete accountability system. Of course, a physical wouldn't be complete without blood pressure tests; they are one piece of a larger puzzle. So it is with test scores. Good accountability systems should include several measures of student achievement, including not only test scores but also other evaluations of student work, including evaluations of student writing, collections of student work, and appraisals of student proficiency conducted by the classroom teacher and independent evaluators.

2. It should have information about the underlying causes of student achievement. This includes a wide variety of other variables, but at the very least it would include information about student attendance, teacher certification, and curriculum. After all, if a student misses school half the time or arrives in a school only a few weeks before the test is administered, such a test is not an accurate reflection of that teacher's work or the curriculum of that school. Similarly, if a student is in a classroom with an unqualified teacher and is using a curriculum that is unrelated to the test, then few accurate conclusions can be drawn about the ability of that student. In the best accountability systems, these underlying causes of student achievement include not only attendance and teacher data but also a host of other school-based variables that reflect the educational strategies of different schools. When these variables are studied, researchers can learn what strategies are most effective for improving student achievement.

3. It should have a mix of qualitative and quantitative information. It is certainly possible that two schools could have very similar test scores and yet be vastly different places of learning. The use of a brief narrative to describe

the school climate and other factors influencing student achievement in each school would allow those who read accountability reports to better understand the "story behind the numbers."

I have elaborated on the creation of accountability systems in my book, *Accountability in Action: A Blueprint for Learning Organizations*, 2nd Edition (2004). Sample chapters are available for free on our web site at www.LeadandLearn.com.

76 How do I find out if my school already has an accountability system?

Every school system in existence has some sort of accountability system, though many of these systems are unnamed and clandestine. I would start with personnel evaluation practices. What are the criteria by which teachers and school leaders are hired, retained, promoted, or dismissed? In addition, review the minutes of the superintendent's cabinet and the board of education. What are the information sources used for those leaders and policy makers to render their decisions? Every school system has an accountability system of some sort, whether or not it bears that name. The advantage of a clearly stated accountability system is that the "rules of the game" become clear. Moreover, the establishment of a clear and open accountability system will force the school system to confront the mixed messages that prevail when there is an implicit accountability system without clearly defined information sources, expectations, and requirements.

77 Accountability is a scary word. If I am to be accountable for something, then shouldn't I have control over those things I am accountable for?

Yes. This is the very reason that we believe that "accountability is more than test scores." Moreover, we advocate principles of accountability that include this very issue: Those being held accountable must have influence over those factors for which they are held accountable. Exhorting teachers to "Raise test scores!" is unhelpful unless we provide specific instructional strategies that are associated with improved achievement. For example, we know that when teachers use frequent non-fiction writing assessments with collaborative scoring, students are very likely to have improved test scores. Such a rise in test scores is never guaranteed; it is simply very likely. Therefore, measuring test scores alone is not nearly as effective as measuring what the teacher can control, such as the frequency of non-fiction writing assessments with collaborative scoring. In this way (and many others), accountability can be effective and fair, measuring things that teachers are directly responsible for. Such a multiple-measure accountability system also makes it clear that high scores alone are not the definitions of "success" unless the school is also improving its strategies in instruction, curriculum, and leadership.

Expecting the Best

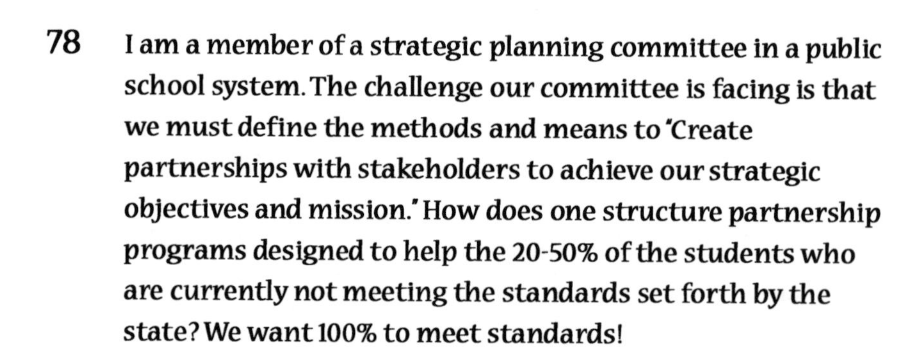

78 I am a member of a strategic planning committee in a public school system. The challenge our committee is facing is that we must define the methods and means to 'Create partnerships with stakeholders to achieve our strategic objectives and mission.' How does one structure partnership programs designed to help the 20-50% of the students who are currently not meeting the standards set forth by the state? We want 100% to meet standards!

I applaud your goal of "100%." If you fail to set such a goal, then you will guarantee that the students not meeting standards receive an excuse rather than assistance. That said, it is a reality that a significant number of students do not meet the standard. What do you do for them? Here are some preliminary ideas:

1. *Diagnose* early and often. You simply cannot deal with a problem until you have diagnosed it. Examination of statewide test scores is too late. Every teacher should be able to answer these questions: How many of my students meet state academic standards? How many times have I assessed them on their proficiency in meeting those standards? I do not wish to imply that every single standard must be tested every month, but a few critically important standards—the "power standards" such as math problem-solving, nonfiction writing, reading comprehension—must be tested at least monthly. If these students were in the intensive care ward of a hospital, how frequently would their vital signs be measured? Perhaps the best way to communicate the imperative for meaningful classroom assessment is this analogy: You must decide if you are going to conduct an autopsy or a physical. Annual state tests are autopsies; frequent classroom-based assessments are physicals. The former tells us how the patient died; the latter tell us how to improve.

2. *Intervene* swiftly and with certainty. If students cannot read their 8th grade social studies textbook, must we wait until May to flunk them and notice that there is a problem? Surely we can intervene now, providing intensive instruction in literacy early in the school year. I recognize that this implies changing carefully thought-out schedules and protocols. To every such objection, I would only ask, "How inconvenient is it if you wait until this child is in even more trouble?"

3. *Re-allocate* resources. You cannot do #2 above without resources, and in every school system, resources are limited. This might mean that we give lower class sizes to the teachers willing to have 3rd graders who can't read and 8th graders who can't compute. That implies higher class sizes for Advanced Placement Calculus. So be it. You will have more volunteers for the latter than for the former.

4. *Stick to* your goals. Failure is not an option. Give to every student in the district the individual attention and incremental goals you give to your special education students and most gifted students.

79 Our school is preparing for our state accountability program. I am trying to design a road map that will help our school be very effective as we plan for the new year. Can you help?

Most state departments of education do have specific procedures for the planning documents that they require, but let me offer some practical advice for the procedures I would consider at the school and classroom level for using data to improve learning and teaching:

1. *Look at the data*. Go beyond test scores and look at everything from standardized tests to teacher-made tests to grades to attendance to parent involvement. What do the data tell you about your school community? Where are the consistencies ("We clearly are strong in this area, not so strong here...")? Where are the inconsistencies ("40% of the students on the honor roll are not proficient writers; we must be sending mixed messages to those kids"). Before you do anything, start with the facts.

2. *Identify your strengths*. Go to the sub-scales (not the average test scores) and find at least two or three areas where your teachers and students are doing a terrific job. Be as specific as possible. Don't say "reading," but rather, "We're really great at reading strategies," or "We're terrific at vocabulary building for ESL students." Then ask this critical question: "What are we doing as a staff in these highly successful areas that we are not doing in areas where the same kids are not as successful?" My experience is that you will hear things like, "We focus more," or "We spend more time," or "We do that in almost every grade," or "We do that in many different places in the curriculum." In other words, the solution to improvement need not be externally generated, but is a product of thoughtful reflection on what is already working in your school.

3. *Identify your challenges*. Again, specificity is essential. Don't say, "We need to be better in math." Instead, say, "Our

students appear to be particularly weak in measurement and in graphs."

4. *Develop specific strategies*, based on your analysis of your strengths (#2), to address your challenges. For example: "Our analysis of our strengths indicated that we were really good in shapes and patterns because students learn this in math and art. Perhaps we should take the same approach to our weaknesses in measurement and plan specific measurement units not only in math but also in art and physical education."

5. *Measure your results*. Don't just post test scores once a year; measure the degree to which you are implementing your strategies. Then measure the percentage of your students that are "proficient" or better at the most critical standards you have identified.

80 I am very concerned that my school system is publicly posturing itself to be politically correct, but silently agonizing over unrealistic expectations. As our superintendent said, 'Who is going to volunteer their children to not meet the standard? That is why we must have 100% of them meeting goals.'

Let us be clear about the reason that "100%" is an appropriate goal. It has nothing to do with being politically correct or looking good. It has everything to do with giving every student the opportunity for success that they deserve. We must also be clear about what this objective means: 100% achieving goals does not mean 100% achieving them on precisely the same day. That doesn't happen in any district on earth. In a standards-based system, *time* is the variable, not achievement. In practice, this means that some of your students will need an extra year of high school; some will need an extra hour of grade school; some will need an extra eight weeks before middle school. Parents of college-age children routinely acknowledge this reality for their children. What makes us think that kids are perfectly linear and scheduled from K-12, then are non-linear in college and, of course, pre-school? Stick to your good goal, just don't define it as everyone doing the same standard at the same time. Remember, time, not achievement, is the variable.

Accountability for All

81 **How do you convince teachers to implement curriculum in a district accountability system?**

The central issue is not "convincing" professionals to do what is right, but rather to identify clearly and objectively when people fail to do what is necessary and right.

Why should educators implement the standards-based curriculum in your district? There are only two reasons: fairness and effectiveness. I've elaborated on this theme in Part One of my book, *Making Standards Work* (2002), and many other authors (Mitchell, 1992; Rothman, 1995; Wiggins, 1998) have addressed it as well. If a professional does not choose to do something that is fair and effective, then "convincing" doesn't work. It is like trying to "convince" a school nurse that vaccinations are a good idea, or convincing a school safety officer that a gun in a backpack is a bad idea. After you have presented the research and the evidence, the policy and the tools, then we implement it.

That brings us to the heart of the matter. How do we use accountability to insure appropriate implementation of a standards-based curriculum? This is not a conversation about *whether* to implement a sound idea. In every great movement, there are people who don't like the change, either because it is a change or because they disagree with it philosophically (just ask the people who were school administrators in 1954 after the Brown v. Board of Education decision). The point is that our mission is not the care and comfort of the adults in the system, and the fact that some people give you a hard time about your commitment to equity and excellence is not a reason to stop your excellent leadership or even break your stride. The accountability system should evaluate the student work on the assessments in the classroom. Do the assessments used by the teacher support the standards? Do the curriculum, units, and activities used by the teacher support the standards? These are objective questions with clear responses, and if the answers are in the negative, then it is not a matter of "academic freedom." It is, rather, as if a teacher disagreed with safety or health regulations in the school. The teacher is entitled to his or her opinion, but that does not negate the appropriate implementation and enforcement of those regulations. If your community would not tolerate a nurse who refused to administer vaccinations, then why would you tolerate a teacher who refused to help students learn to read and otherwise meet your standards? Both, I submit, are issues affecting the future health of the children in the district.

82 I don't think anyone fears accountability if they are free to address those things in the venture that determine the outcome. But, if I have to act and react a predetermined way that my instincts argue against, when I know a way to dodge and duck and connect with a disadvantaged student, am I doing the right thing by the child, but the wrong thing by regulations?

"Doing the right thing" is laudable, but we have to have a clear understanding of what that means. I've encountered way too many people who have thrown in the towel on disadvantaged students because of their conviction that "they can't do the work required of them." An astonishing number of educators appear to believe that expecting disadvantaged students to meet high academic standards will hurt the self-esteem of those students.

I cannot infer from your question what a "connection" with the student means. If this connection were associated with a genuine love and interest, along with high expectations and demands for performance (even at the risk of making the student angry now and then), then I would endorse your approach. But if "connection" means that we are reluctant to place high demands on students of whom too little has been asked in the past, then I must dissent. It is not the job of the successful educator, coach, orchestra leader, or algebra teacher to befriend their students at the expense of the student's future. We must, rather, have the confidence to risk short-term discontent and challenge in order to achieve the results we know are possible, indeed essential, for the students we serve.

Q 83 Because the test scores in my district are reported in their totality, there is no accounting for the kids who came to us right before the test was taken. I don't think it's fair that I'm being held accountable for the test scores of students whom I have only taught for two weeks! How can I make this reporting more fair and accurate?

A An important requirement of any accountability system is that it is accurate. Consider this analogy. In pharmaceutical tests, we compare the patients in the control group to patients in the experimental group. Those people in the control group took a sugar pill, or placebo, and the patients in the experimental group took the real pills. If we are going to accurately understand the impact of the pharmaceutical, what do we need to know about the patients in the experimental group? That they really took the pills. If they showed up to the experiment just a few days before the end and hadn't taken any of the pills, then the doctors cannot make an accurate comparison between the control group and the experimental group.

In education, it makes no sense to evaluate schools, curricula, teachers, students, or programs based on students who "didn't take the pill"; students who were not present in school while the instruction was taking place. Therefore, it is essential that schools sort and report their test data as follows:

1. Scores for all students taking the test.

2. Scores for students who attended school 90% of the time and were continuously enrolled for the previous eight months.

3. Scores for students who attended school 90% of the time and were continuously enrolled for fewer than the previous eight months.

4. Scores for students who were continuously enrolled, but who attended school less than 90% of the time.

Only in this way can school leaders gain an accurate understanding of the impact of teaching on student achievement. I have seen many schools who take this a step further and analyze the scores of students who have been continuously enrolled in their district for one, two, three, or four years. In this way, they hope to demonstrate that the longer students stay with the district, the better their achievement.

Your question raises another important issue. What is the best way to deal with highly mobile students and with students who come to a school right before a test? In the most effective schools we have observed, principals and teachers invest a great deal of time, sometimes several days, getting to know students and their parents, learning about prior educational experiences, and performing extensive diagnostic assessments. This gives the student the opportunity to become socialized to a small group of adults and students before going to the classroom. This approach also gives the teacher the opportunity to begin a relationship with a student with some background knowledge about the student's education, prior learning, and academic skills.

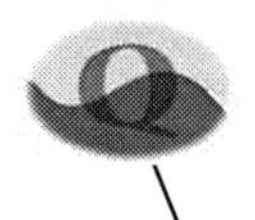

84 What legal actions can be taken to get parents to be accountable for their children?

In cases of abuse and neglect, legal remedies exist, and in most states, educational authorities have an obligation to report such cases to appropriate authorities. But I suspect you are referring not to cases of abuse and neglect, but to cases in which children come to school without having discussed their homework with a parent, without having notes and letters signed by parents, or without having parents in the home who exhibit any sort of interest in the child's education. Chances are, these parents were themselves alienated from school, and you are now paying the price for the bad experiences of those parents. Some practices you might want to consider include the following:

1. Call the parents with "Good News" reports. Many parents have been conditioned to think that any call from the school is bad news and should be avoided. "I just wanted to tell you that Jerome did a great job in reading today..." It might be your phone call that eventually breaks the ice.

2. Change the location of parent-teacher meetings. One school I've worked with meets parents in a local shopping mall. Another meets parents in a church basement. Find a "safe" place that parents can regard as neutral territory. Teachers can then approach parents as colleagues and partners, not as authority figures who are lecturing the parents about the failings of their children.

3. Invite parents to help create scenarios for learning activities and assessments. The "real world" parents' home, recreation, and career can help make assessments and assignments real, relevant, and meaningful to children. It also shows respect for the contribution parents can make to their child's learning.

85 How, in terms of test responses, can a teacher be held accountable for what another person chooses or doesn't choose to do?

Teachers do not make the marks in the test booklets, but teachers certainly determine the extent to which they have used instructional and assessment practices that help prepare students to do well on tests. A good accountability system will consider not merely the test scores, but the actual activities in which teachers have engaged. Let us be clear about the research on this point: Teaching matters. It is simply not accurate to contend that teachers are impotent bystanders while students choose to act or fail to act. While I do not underestimate the importance of student motivation and the power of their individual free will, the overwhelming evidence indicates that the quality of the teacher is the single largest ingredient in student achievement, including student performance on tests (see Kati Haycock's splendid articles available at the Education Trust web site, www.edtrust.org, and William Sanders' articles available at www.sasinschool.com).

It is not teachers alone who bear responsibility here. Administrators who routinely assign our most qualified and experienced teachers to the least needy classrooms, and assign our least qualified and experienced teachers to the most needy classrooms, are guilty of grave inequities. Boards that tolerate a "seniority" system of assigning teachers in which experience and quality in teaching will migrate away from poor kids to rich kids must also be held accountable. Thus teachers, administrators, and boards of education all bear responsibility here, as do the students and parents.

There are several practical things we can do in order to make accountability fair and meaningful. First, we must use a multiple measure accountability system that includes not only test scores, but the teaching and leadership behaviors at work in the system. Second, we must have consequences for students based on their performance in the classroom. If a student is not proficient in reading, then their schedule and curriculum must be directed in such a way that proficiency becomes much more likely. Only in this way can accountability move away from a destructive force used for political ends to a constructive force that leads to improved opportunities for students.

CHAPTER

9

90/90/90 Schools

All Students Can Achieve

86 What is a 90/90/90 school? What is the significance of these schools?

The 90/90/90 schools are quite unusual because their student populations include at least 90% free and reduced lunch students, 90% minority students, and 90% or more of students who meet or exceed state academic standards. We initially found these schools, and developed the label "90/90/90," in Milwaukee, Wisconsin. Since that time, we have joined a number of other researchers in documenting the success of schools with a high percentage of poor and minority students. After visiting many of these schools, we found that they had several characteristics in common:

1. They shared a *laser-like focus on student achievement*, an issue that dominated every faculty meeting, staff development presentation, and even the casual discussions among teachers and administrators. Among the many visible indicators of this laser-like focus was the school trophy case in which examples of exemplary student work could be found. Any visitor to these schools was struck by the clear and visible emphasis that was placed on academic success.

2. These schools *emphasized student writing*, with weekly writing assessments and a common scoring guide, or rubric, to provide clear feedback on student performance. In particular, we noticed an emphasis on non-fiction writing, a genre frequently under-emphasized in many other schools.

3. The teachers routinely *collaborated on scoring* so that they were able to give consistent feedback to the students. This collaboration was consistent and widespread. Teachers used every opportunity, such as casual conversation, formal staff development, faculty meetings, and planning time, to

focus on real student work and collaborate about their expectations for student performance.

4. Students were afforded *multiple opportunities* to succeed on assignments. The consequence of a student failing to meet a standard was not a low grade but rather the opportunity to respect the feedback of the teacher and re-submit the assignment.

Since these original observations were made, the number of 90/90/90 schools has expanded not only in Milwaukee but also around the nation.

The significance of the 90/90/90 schools is that they collectively make clear that the demographic characteristics of students do not predict the destiny of those students. While poverty, language, and ethnicity may have had some relationship to student achievement in previous studies, it is a grave error when policy makers, educational leaders, and teachers presume that we should have lower expectations of students because of their socioeconomic status or ethnic heritage. The students and teachers of the 90/90/90 schools make clear that challenges of home and neighborhood are not reasons to have lower expectations in schools. Most importantly, these schools make clear that specific and replicable teaching and leadership behaviors can have an enormous impact on student achievement.

Q 87 **When looking at grades and test scores, shouldn't the background of the student be taken into consideration? What if he/she is doing his/her best and is making progress, but does not achieve what we have defined as advanced work? Don't they deserve credit?**

A I'm not sure what is meant by "background," but this is frequently a code word for poverty, ethnicity, or language. My frank answer is, "No, this should not be taken into consideration, because when we do so, we are saying that we have lower expectations of some students based on their appearance or economic status." As a teacher, I understand that poverty influences student achievement, but the evidence is overwhelming that demographic variables are less than half as influential as effective teaching.

88 **Every year, I have several kids in my class who, I can tell, come from poor and sometimes difficult homes. It is always difficult for me to demand the same expectations of them as the other kids, because it is clear to me that they have so many other things to think about. Kids today are certainly forced to deal with so many more problems than my generation did! Is it wrong to let my compassion for their underprivileged circumstances cause me to give them a break?**

First, let me express my appreciation for the compassion and caring for students that so clearly is contained in your question. Many teachers would find another building or class as quickly as possible and would not continue to face the challenges you have chosen to accept. Therefore, I frame this response with deep respect for a professional who clearly cares about the students in your classes, and part of that deep respect is candor. The plain fact is that you do your students no favor when you wish to "give them a break" in the form of lower academic expectations. While it is true that students from challenging social and home environments need your love and concern, they do not need one more adult presuming that they are incapable of doing great work.

How can you balance your intuitive desire to be sensitive to the needs of these students with the clear professional mandate we all share to maintain high expectations of all students? Here are some guidelines you may wish to consider.

1. Evaluate achievement, not time. This means that when students don't turn in homework on time or produce an unacceptable work product, the response is neither to fail them nor to "give them a break" by accepting unsatisfactory work. The answer is to make time, rather than your expectations, the variable. In extreme cases

where the work remains incomplete at the end of the semester, this may mean that you give the honest grade of "incomplete." You do not fail the student, but you don't pass them on to the next class with a "D" or a "C" when you know that they are headed for failure when a teacher, employer, professor, or graduation test administrator finally confronts them with the truth. By evaluating achievement rather than time, you give students multiple opportunities for success and you express a willingness to vary your strategies as well as your expectations for the time required to complete an assignment. But you do not lower your academic requirements based on home life or other circumstances.

2. Provide multi-task assessments. Some of the students you describe need your individual assistance. That becomes an impossibility when every student is working on the same task at the same time. In fact, students process information at different paces and their learning backgrounds are strikingly different. By using multi-task assessments (my rule of thumb is a minimum of four tasks per assessment), you allow some students to proceed quickly through the first two or three tasks, and then face a serious challenge that slows them down on the fourth task. Other students may be struggling with the first two tasks. The multi-task assessment approach allows you to spend more time in small groups or with individual students who need your coaching and assistance. Of course, this also implies that you are doing much less whole-group instruction and hardly any lecturing to the entire class. Please see Chapter 3 on Performance Assessments for more information on the subject.

3. Provide for multiple opportunities for success. The students you describe have been discouraged by a system that insists that their first submission of schoolwork represents their only opportunity for success. Because, as you noted, they may not have help at home and have little encouragement toward success, these students need to use teacher feedback as a source of improved achievement, not merely as a source of evaluation and

grades. Frankly, this is a great technique for all students, regardless of their home circumstances or demographic characteristics.

The essence of your question is a request for authorization to expect less of some kids based on their economic, family, or other personal circumstances. However tempting that may be and however sympathetic the motives associated with such lower expectations, we dare not allow ourselves as educators to go down that path. If we do so, we are trading a few moments of the pleasure of having pleased a student for a lifetime of regret. While they will rarely thank you at the time, students need your high expectations and your "unreasonable" demands for great performance. Despite their pleas and protests, they do not need you to expect less of them than you would of the most economically advantaged student that you serve.

The Research Behind the Numbers

89 What research supports the 90/90/90 study, and what do those schools have in common?

You might want to read my book, *Accountability in Action*, 2nd Edition (2004). It contains additional details on the 90/90/90 schools. You can download the chapter about those schools for free at www.LeadandLearn.com. In addition, let me recommend Haycock, Barth, Jackson, Mora, Ruiz, Robinson, and Wilkins' excellent publication, "Dispelling the Myth" (1999). You can download it from www.edtrust.org. Go to "publications" and select the titles you would like.

As you are no doubt aware, these two studies are a tiny fraction of the literature on achievement in high poverty schools that also have high percentages of minority students. There are some common characteristics of successful schools in high poverty areas. These characteristics include:

1. *Focus*. Literacy and mathematics are more important than other things. If a student comes to 9th grade with a 4th grade reading level, that student needs more than one hour a day of literacy. The only options are more time or the simple acknowledgment that literacy is more important than other classes. The notion that there is a magic textbook, program, or technological initiative that will allow students to "work smarter" and thus acquire six years of literacy education in one hour a day is nonsense. Please see Chapter 7 for other interventions for underperforming students.

2. *Writing*. An increasing number of state tests emphasize student writing skills. In particular, students at the secondary level need a greater emphasis on non-fiction writing. The contentions that this essential skill can be replaced with oral reports, magic dictating pens (as I once heard a national speaker assert), or anything else except the critical thinking and cognitive processes entailed in writing are assertions without evidence. Our evidence on the matter, however, is dramatic: Every area tested—math, science, social studies, and language arts—shows increases in student achievement when students write more frequently with teacher feedback and student re-writing.

3. *Collaborative Scoring*. Teachers are the most important variable in student success. It isn't programs or fads. It is teachers who, working collaboratively, provide a clear and consistent picture of acceptable student performance.

90 **I am the principal of an elementary school, and although student achievement is not an issue for us, I believe that we all have much to learn from the 90/90/90 schools. Recently, I read Alfie Kohn's book, *The Schools Our Children Deserve* (1999), and I have been engaged in a personal professional struggle about how to make it all work. In a perfect world, I agree with Kohn on what constitutes good teaching and learning, but I know our realities, too. I need to restore balance to our ongoing debate about how to make**

standards doable. I would appreciate a recommendation about material that could be used both at my school site and the district level about the 90/90/90 schools.

Although I don't share Kohn's more extreme positions on boycotting tests and dismantling standards, I endorse some of his observations about effective teaching practice. The appendices to his book are excellent, and I particularly appreciate the contrast he makes between an effective and an ineffective classroom. The "constructive chaos" of small groups, differentiated instruction, and multiple learning opportunities are what we would both recommend. That said, Kohn's suggestion that the only way teachers can have improved test scores is through stultifying test drills and the elimination of teaching based on reasoning, thinking, and communication is not supported by the evidence. Great teaching, which includes a focus on thinking, reasoning, and communication, is associated with higher, not lower, test scores.

You asked for some additional resources beyond Alfie Kohn. You might consider several sources. Linda Darling-Hammond's excellent book, *The Right to Learn* (1997), would be a good general book study. She offers a mountain of evidence on effective teaching and assessment. On the specifics of creating effective and engaging classroom assessments, you may want to review my book, *Making Standards Work* (2002). To get models of good assessments, you might want to check our web site at www.LeadandLearn.com, where you can download free sample assessments. Finally, on the specifics of the 90/90/90 schools to which you referred in your question, check out chapter 19 of *Accountability in Action*, 2nd Edition (2004). You can download that chapter for free from www.LeadandLearn.com as well.

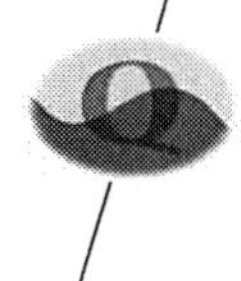

91 I have heard you say that demographics account for 24% of the variability in student test scores, but teacher factors (expertise, training, experience) account for 49% of the variability. A colleague showed me some information on a

study by Professor John Pikulski. His research said "home and family factors" account for 49% of student achievement; "teacher qualifications" accounted for 43%; and class size was 8%. Without even looking at the family/ teacher factors, I knew that class size claim was completely bogus. Based on your studies, I thought that Pikulski's home and family factors might be overstated. Would you say the 24/49 correlation applies for all populations or just students in the 90/90/90 studies? Do you have a source I can reference that explains the 24/49 variability factor?

A I'm not familiar with the study that you cite, but I am quite familiar with different multivariate analyses showing strikingly different findings. Back in the days of the Coleman report (still widely cited and mis-cited), people believed that they could "prove" that demographics were more than 80% of student achievement. More recently, *The Bell Curve* authors Herrnstein and Murray (1994) made similar claims about genetic heritage. The information I cited (Darling-Hammond, 1997; and Darling-Hammond & Sykes, 1998) obviously comes to a different conclusion. How can policy makers and leaders sort out who is right? You certainly don't need a statistics lecture from me, but let me offer some ideas that you might want to share with colleagues should the issue arise:

1. Multivariate equations are only as good as the variables they contain and the accuracy of their measurement. Many studies that claim large impacts of demographics and genetics *do not measure* teacher certification, subject-matter qualification, and other indicators of quality. If you don't measure it, you aren't likely to find many effects.

2. No single study, including those I have conducted, is ever definitive. That's why I ask you to consider multiple sources. Some of those you might want to consult include Kati Haycock (www.edtrust.org), William Sanders (www.sasinschool.com), and Linda Darling-Hammond (numerous publications, but most clearly in *The Right to Learn*,

1997). The cumulative weight of evidence, including my 90/90/90 studies (which you can also download for free at www.LeadandLearn.com, indicates that the old argument that demographics are determinative is not substantiated. In the latest accountability report from the 90/90/90 schools (Milwaukee Public Schools, 2000), there are more schools on the list, indicating that the practices are replicable. There are striking improvements in social studies, science, math, and reading, all of which are associated with increased levels of writing and performance assessment, just as the earlier data had indicated.

3. We need to consider seriously the key question facing leaders and policy makers: Given that there is uncertainty, what is the best course of action? Do we wait for the perfect study, or consider the cumulative weight of evidence and use our best judgment to improve opportunities for students? What the impact is of the argument if I'm wrong? What if, for example, teaching quality is "only" 43% rather than 49%? What if demographics were 80% and teaching practice were only 20%? What if teacher assessment and writing practices in the classroom don't raise achievement as much as my studies indicate, but only gives them a slight advantage in communication skills? My argument would be that teachers and leaders are obligated to consider the weight of the evidence and not wait for perfection in research. What we know for sure is that student achievement isn't where we want it to be, and that there are some techniques, such as using subject-matter certified teachers, increasing student writing with consistent scoring guides, and giving students opportunities to respect teacher feedback and improve their work, that are effective in improving achievement. The possibility that there are other variables in the mix should never deter us from doing the best we can with the time and talents that we have.

Methods That Work

92 What other instructional methods have been implemented in these 90/90/90 schools? Writing alone won't fix everything. There still has to be other instruction going on. How is it being done?

This is certainly true. The 90/90/90 schools use many effective techniques, but one consistently effective technique stands out as particularly powerful: frequent non-fiction writing assessments with consistent scoring guides and collaborative scoring. Most schools simply don't do as much writing, or as many writing assessments, as these effective schools do. Other techniques used in effective high poverty schools include frequent monitoring of student progress, intensive intervention for students who need additional help in literacy and math, personal involvement by the principal in a student assessment, and the use of common scoring rubrics for all students in a grade.

93 I first heard about the 90/90/90 schools a couple of years ago. Have they been able to sustain their high performance since then? Are they still as good as they used to be, or was this achievement more of a one-time occurrence?

Since you first heard the data a couple of years ago, we have new information that is even more encouraging about these schools. First, the number of 90/90/90 schools has significantly increased, indicating that the practices we originally observed in those schools are replicable. Second, the predominant assessment practices associated with the 90/90/90 schools, namely increases in non-fiction writing and performance assessment, are associated with significant increases in multiple choice test scores in reading, language arts, science, social studies, and math. Third, the results continue to be in evidence in middle and high school.

None of the 90/90/90 schools were part of vouchers or charters; all were regular public schools. It is also true that many of the more than 200 schools in Milwaukee are very troubled and the school board has been notoriously fractious. Nevertheless, amidst the chaos, the 90/90/90 schools have continued to thrive for several consecutive years, even as poverty and minority enrollment remains very high.

Finally, and most important, the 90/90/90 schools we have documented are certainly not the only examples of great success in high poverty schools. You can find very similar research at www.edtrust.org and at www.heritage.org, both of which provide studies that independently confirm our findings.

94 I have been reading some of your information on 90/90/90 schools. I will be principal of a middle school next year that is in a community that is filled with drug dealers, prostitution, and meth labs. What are some steps I can take to turn it into a 90/90/90 school?

Here are some ideas for you to consider:

1. *Professional Development*. Determine the knowledge and skills that the faculty and leaders in your school will require. Whether they are new teachers or veterans, possessing multiple certificates or emergency credentials, there are some basic knowledge and skills that all of them need. The leader must identify those criteria and choose teacher-leaders who can take a modeling and leadership responsibility in each area. My candidates for this knowledge and skills list would include:

   a. Classroom management

   b. Student assessment with particular emphasis on diagnostic assessment

   c. Curriculum focus: taking the state standards and school textbooks and narrowing the focus to specific "safety net" skills for each class

d. Assessment design: creating engaging and specific performance assessments that are linked to necessary skills

e. Multiple intelligences: integrating physical education, art, and music into the core academic requirements of the school.

2. *Focus*. As the leader, you make clear that you respect and value the experiences, backgrounds, and diverse viewpoints of your teachers. That richness of experience will be essential to meet the needs of children. There are, however, core values on which they cannot have a diversity of beliefs. These include matters such as safety (everybody will have a safe environment in which to learn and teach) and high expectations (every adult in the system will maintain high expectations of every child, with those expectations defined solely by our academic standards, and not by skin color, family background, or socioeconomic status). No amount of staff development in the world will change racism, and if you have people who do not believe that children of color or poor children can learn, you must find a way to move them elsewhere. It is just as serious as if you had a teacher who said that she personally believed that kids taking guns to school was a fine idea. She can hold those beliefs, but not in your school.

3. *Collaboration*. Directly related to the area of focus is collaboration. Many leaders talk about collaboration, but their actions belie their words. The acid test of effective collaboration is how you conduct faculty meetings and staff development. These are collaborative only when teachers bring student work along and the group, whether it is the entire faculty or a few teachers from a single grade level, collaborates on the evaluation of that work. The goal is to have a clear focus on what "proficiency" means. In addition, teachers can systematically reflect on their professional practice. What worked? What did not work? How can we improve this lesson next week?

4. *Track progress frequently*. When you are starting with low test scores, don't make people wait until next year to get some positive feedback. Identify a very few core skills, such as reading comprehension, informative writing, and tables/charts/graphs. Decide on a level of proficiency for each one of these, and create assessments. By the end of September, create a chart for the whole school (not one class pitted against another) that shows the percentage of students proficient or better. It will be grim, perhaps 10 or 20%, if your standards are set right and the grading is collaborative and accurate. But you'll do it again in October, November, etc. When you hit 90%, have a party; when you hit 100%, do something very special. This makes three important points:

    a. We are *not* last year's test scores

    b. We are getting better *every* day

    c. We may not all learn at the same rate, pace, and time, but we will *all* learn before this year is over.

You can expect to run into a thousand objections, many of which center on the thesis that children of poverty can't do this. To some extent, I hope that my research, as well as the other research I cite (see www.edtrust.org and www.heritage.org) makes the case very plain that high poverty, high minority, and high achieving schools are possible and increasingly common. But I must tell you that I answer angry e-mails every week about this research, and though I do reply to them, it's quite clear that the questioners don't want a reply. They just want to espouse the theory that poor children cannot succeed. A few of them are the "honest racists" who are so blatant about their point of view that they ask, "If everybody meets standards, then who will take out the garbage?" More than a few of these people, whether or not they are that blatant, carry teaching certificates, have tenure, and can talk a good game about caring for children. You can't change them. They are bigots and a cancer in your faculty, and you need to get rid of them or get them reassigned to a position that does not involve contact with children. I would literally rather have larger class sizes than I would have a faculty that includes people who believe my children cannot learn.

95 How can we keep effective teachers working with poor students?

A recent Public Agenda survey suggests that money alone is not the answer (2000). Although 75% of teachers either "strongly agree" or "somewhat agree" with the statement, "I am seriously underpaid," more than 86% of the respondents said that they would rather work in a school with a lower salary where student behavior and parental support were significantly higher. More than 73% of administrators felt the same way: Student behavior and parental support were more important than increased salary. Teachers require not only fair and reasonable compensation, but safety, fairness, and an understanding of the demands of their work environment.

So what do we do to encourage teachers to work in the nation's poorest schools? I would consider a variety of non-economic incentives, including reduced class sizes and extra planning periods for teachers who are willing to work with our most challenging students. In addition, administrators in all schools, including those in the poorest and most challenging neighborhoods, have an absolute responsibility to students and employees to maintain a safe and orderly environment. Finally, school leaders can provide teachers with training, advanced educational opportunities, professional respect, and, of course, significantly improved economic incentives to enter and remain in the educational profession.

CHAPTER

10

Leadership Issues

The Many Facets of Leadership

96 How can I be more effective as a leader?

First, let's define what leaders do and why we need them. If every system were simply on auto-pilot and every member of the system did precisely the right things at the right time based on the right information, leaders would be irrelevant. Unfortunately, I've never seen such an organization. We need leaders, regardless of whether we like them or want them.

As a brief summary, we can start our unending journey toward effective leadership with three steps:

1. *Focus* on vision. Leaders must be a "broken record" of articulating the clear vision. In school, it might be "excellence and equity for all." It is clear, compelling, and unambiguous. But because so few people really share that vision at first, try to spend every meeting, private and public, articulating and repeating that vision.

2. *Learn* what the organization really does. That means a lot of listening and examination of data. I am continually stunned by the number of leaders, including principals and central office people, who simply do not know what is going on in the schools. I'll ask, "What will the staff development calendar be for next year?" or, "What is the curriculum plan for students who are not proficient readers?" and I receive a vacant stare and some generalities about such matters really being a site-based issue. Leaders must know what the organization does.

3. *Concentrate* the attention of the organization on the most important tasks. This is not merely a recitation of a "to do" list. In fact, the most important part of focusing on the right tasks is the difficult and unpopular job of identifying things *not* to do. Effective academic leaders do not merely say, "More reading." They facilitate a conversation in which

teachers collaboratively identify chapters of the textbook *not* to address, curriculum areas that can be dropped, and units, activities, and time-wasters that must be eliminated. Leaders set the example by eliminating things, including unfocused meetings, irrelevant staff development, meaningless assemblies, and mindless intercom announcements, for which administrators are the most common source.

4. *Provide feedback* in a continuous loop of reinforcement, encouragement, and coaching.

If you wish to explore beyond the boundaries of traditional school administration, I would consider the work of Bennis (2000), Peters and Waterman (1988), Wheatley (1999), and Drucker (1999) as interesting sources for the further study of effective leadership.

97 We want our teachers to be serious about standards and assessment. Can our teacher evaluation forms play a role in doing this?

A primary consideration is that the teacher evaluation forms should not send mixed messages. For example, some districts have a standards program that encourages a focus on a few core standards, yet they still use a teacher evaluation form that implies that teachers must "cover the curriculum" in order to receive a satisfactory evaluation.

For optimal effectiveness, a teacher evaluation form is used as a coaching device. In the classroom, an effective scoring guide, or rubric, can be used not merely to evaluate students but also to help them understand how to improve their performance. Similarly, an effective standards-based teacher evaluation form can be used not only to evaluate teachers, but also to describe a continuum of performance from "exemplary" to "not meeting standards" so that teachers understand in very specific terms how to improve their performance. These evaluation forms typically identify various domains of teaching (classroom management, assessment, instructional planning) and then describe a range of performance for each domain. A teacher might be "proficient" in the domain of assessment based on meeting this requirement:

> This educator routinely uses performance assessments based on state academic standards. Students have multiple opportunities to become proficient on each task. Grades have a clear relationship to the achievement of standards. Students and parents understand what the standards are and how they are used to assess student performance.

A teacher might be "exemplary" in the domain of assessment based on meeting this requirement:

> This educator meets all of the performance requirements for "proficient" performance, and also has achieved the following: The teacher routinely creates new assessments based on our standards and shares those assessments widely with other teachers in the area. This teacher also leads a model classroom that can be used to train other teachers in the creative and appropriate use of standards-based performance assessments. This teacher contributes to the profession by sharing assessments, observations, and techniques in local, regional, and national forums.

Effective teacher evaluation systems *do not*:

- Rank teachers, comparing them against each other
- Provide numerical ratings without clear descriptions of what those ratings mean
- Make judgements about teacher quality based on single tests, or
- Evaluate all teachers as being roughly equal, without clear conclusions about the relative strengths and weaknesses of different professionals.

Leading a Change

98 What are the inhibitors to change?

The primary inhibitor to change is our commitment to comfort. I had a dialog with a colleague recently who remarked how uncomfortable a new role, new projects, and new responsibilities were. "Yes," I responded, "we call that learning." Change, which is what learning certainly is, requires an abandonment of the commitment to comfort. Show me the organization with a mission statement, career goal, or meaningful enterprise that has as its reason for existence "continued, uninterrupted, and infinite comfort," and I will show you a graveyard. If we wish to change, then we must abandon our commitment to comfort. This flies in the face of the image of the school leader as "nurturer" and "caregiver." That is *not* your role. You are there to challenge both adults and students. That does not exclude love, encouragement, and coaching, but you must provide neither love nor respect when you are offered low expectations, excuses, and a litany of reasons why your system, your colleagues, and your students cannot improve.

99 I am the principal of a school that desperately needs to improve student achievement. I have tried to implement some changes, but I still have some teachers who aren't "buying in" to the new ideas. What can I do?

Effective organizational leaders are builders of consensus. Dictatorial schemes don't work and emotional zeal is short-lived. Nevertheless, what do we do with people who can't or won't implement best practices?

I've tried to be pretty candid about my limitations. My inability to "convert the heathen," that is, to magically transform the negative attitudes of recalcitrant teachers and administrators, is at the top of the list. If someone genuinely believes that children cannot succeed, then no amount of rhetoric from me is likely to change that. Nevertheless, I'd like to offer some specific responses to your question about how we convince the most recalcitrant teachers to consider alternative strategies for student success:

1. *Pilot Programs*. People who resist system-wide change may accept a short-term "try before you buy" program. Pilot programs allow the creation of learning laboratories in schools in which alternative strategies (such as increased multidisciplinary writing assessments) can be tried. If the students in those learning labs have better results, let the data speak.

2. *Team Teaching*. When recalcitrant teachers are isolated, we reinforce, rather than challenge, their prejudices. Team teaching allows peer pressure for improved practices to prevail. This is more powerful than administrative pressure.

3. *Action Research*. Create an experiment in which the recalcitrant teachers are empowered, even encouraged, to continue traditional strategies, but with the knowledge that their results will be compared to people using alternative strategies. At the very least, this creates an incentive for all teachers and students to do their best. Perhaps they will "win" and create terrific results for their students. If not, then they have had the opportunity to observe, in a controlled setting, what works and what doesn't. If their methods turn out to be effective or, at the very least, improved as a result of this scrutiny, you have created better opportunities for your students.

4. *Buyouts*. In the rare but real case that you have a teacher who is belligerently incompetent, then you have a straightforward economic decision. Is it cheaper to litigate their dismissal or to buy them out? In most cases, the latter is the more fiscally conservative move. The emotional, economic, and educational toll taken by the belligerent incompetent cannot be sustained. I believe that this is a very tiny percentage of teachers in any district, but it *does* exist. If steps 1-3 are ineffective, then it's time to bite the bullet and terminate their contract. This may involve a

payment to the teacher or payment to attorneys or both. In any event, you need not tolerate the continued presence of someone who is incompetent and harmful to students. An excellent resource on this difficult subject is the book by C. Edward Lawrence, *The Marginal Teacher: A Step-by-step Guide to Fair Procedures for Identification and Dismissal* (1993).

Effective Staff Development

100 We need more professional knowledge on our staff! What are the keys to effective staff development at the school and district level?

First, professional development must be focused on student achievement. That means that every hour and every dollar devoted to professional development should be allocated based on the contribution that such an investment of money and time will make toward improved student achievement. This commitment to focus will exclude many items on the professional development calendar of many school systems.

Second, professional development must meet the needs of individual teachers. Unless your school and district is populated by clones, it is almost never the case that the same professional development program would be appropriate for all staff members. Some teachers may have extensive training in standards and assessment, for example, and they are ready for an advanced course. Other educators may, through no fault of their own, have little or no background knowledge about standards and assessment. Thus, staff development should be a curriculum of different offerings geared toward the needs of the individual teacher, not a calendar that presumes a "one size fits all" approach.

Third, professional development must be evaluated based on its impact on teachers, leaders, and students—not based on its popularity with participants. Many staff development programs are popular; few are effective. Those few programs that provide essential skills for teachers and leaders must be evaluated based on the changes that actually took place in schools. An excellent resource on this subject is *Evaluating Professional Development* by Thomas Guskey (1999).

101 We are narrowing our standards down to "power standards," and we need some advice on how to structure our staff development for the upcoming year to build our school curriculum. Should I ask the teachers to work collaboratively (which is extremely difficult at the high school level), or allow teachers to define their own power standards and then map out curriculum for the year?

It sounds to me as if you need to organize your staff development, but that your high school staff doesn't like to collaborate. Your teachers would prefer to work alone and decide what each one thinks is most important.

Before addressing the issues of staff development, let's consider the fundamental purpose of academic standards. Standards, which are the expectations of what students should know and be able to do, are created in order to communicate clearly, consistently, and fairly to students and parents. The essence of standards is fairness. This does not imply that teachers' opinions are unimportant, but it definitely means that individual opinions of teachers are not definitive. Teaching and curriculum are collaborative decisions in which the state, district, leadership, and teachers all share important roles. Teachers have a great deal of discretion and judgment within the boundaries created by the standards. That is why working on standards, assessment, and curriculum is an inherently collaborative process. In states that do not have academic standards and in districts that are not committed to fairness and consistency, teachers may be free to do whatever they wish, defining instructional effectiveness only through the opinions of individual teachers. But this does not describe any state or district with which I am familiar. For more on standards, please see Chapter 1.

Does the need for collaboration mean that the opinions of teachers should be ignored? Certainly not. Collaboration is not dictation. But teacher judgment and discretion is not anarchy. Most importantly, personal preference and popularity are not the definitive criteria for making decisions about curriculum or staff development.

How can this potentially contentious and difficult issue be handled in practical terms? You must first agree on the basics. What are the criteria that you can use to select power standards? You may disagree on the particulars, but you should be able to agree on the criteria. My suggestions for criteria are these:

1. *Endurance*: Will the knowledge and skills involved in this "power standard" last for years to come?

2. *Leverage*: Do these skills help students in multiple areas of study?

3. *Readiness*: Are these skills necessary for the next level of study?

These criteria help faculty members to focus on the central issues, not on "coverage" of everything that a faculty member believes is important. Moreover, the questions cannot be answered by a single person; they *require* collaboration among different disciplines and different grade levels.

You may want to consult Appendix B, which contains examples of our "power standards" for middle schools. They might help to start the discussion at the high school level.

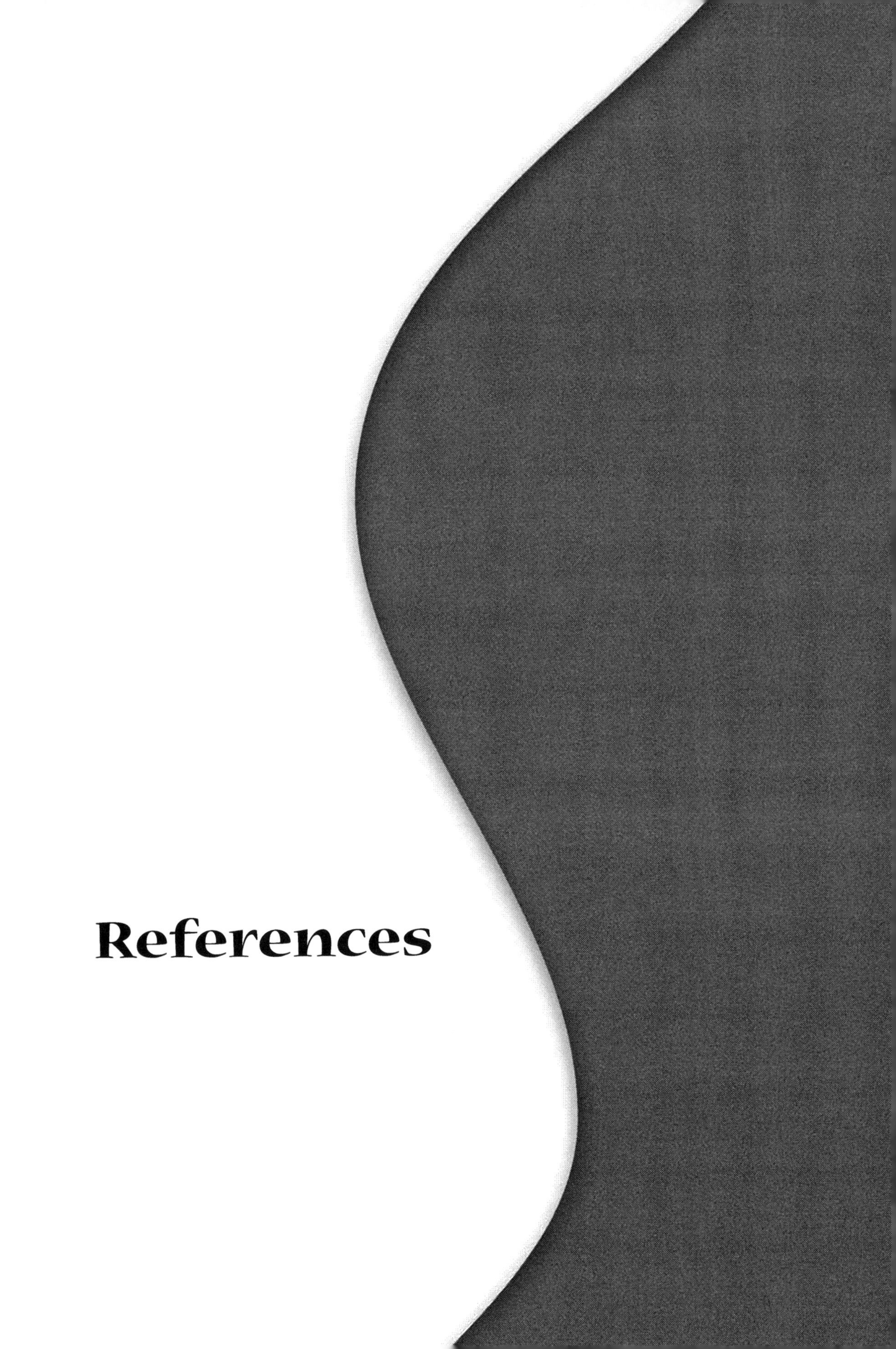

References

Bennis, W. (2000). *Managing the dream: Reflections on leadership and change.* Cambridge, MA: Perseus Publishing.

Campbell, D.G. (1997). *The Mozart effect: Tapping the power of music to heal the body, strengthen the mind, and unlock the creative spirit.* New York: Harper Collins.

Darling-Hammond, L. (1997). *The right to learn.* San Francisco, CA: Jossey-Bass.

Darling-Hammond, L., & Sykes, G. (Eds.). (1998). *Teaching as the learning profession: Handbook of policy and procedure.* San Francisco, CA: Jossey-Bass.

Drucker, P. (1999). *Management challenges for the 21st century.* New York: Harperbusiness.

Gardner, H. (1999). *The disciplined mind: What all students should understand*. New York: Simon & Schuster.

Guskey, T. (1999). *Evaluating professional development.* Thousand Oaks, CA: Sage Publications.

Haycock, K. (1998, Summer). Good teaching matters: How well-qualified teachers can close the gap. *Thinking K-16, A publication of the Education Trust, 3* (2), 1-16.

Haycock, K., Barth, P., Jackson, H., Mora, K., Ruiz, P., Robinson, S., & Wilkins, A. (Eds.). (1999). *Dispelling the myth: High poverty schools exceeding expectations.* Washington, D.C.: The Education Trust.

Herrnstein, R.J. & Murray, C. (1994). *The bell curve: Intelligence and class structure in American life.* New York: The Free Press.

Kohn, A. (1999). *The schools our children deserve: Moving beyond traditional classrooms and "tougher standards."* Boston, MA: Houghton Mifflin.

Language arts grade-level gap. (2000, February). *DataWorks Assessment Newsletter, 2,* (1), p. 1.

Lawrence, C.E. (1993). *The marginal teacher: A step-by-step guide to fair procedures for identification and dismissal*, Thousand Oaks, CA: Corwin Press.

Marzano, R.J. & Kendall, J.S. (1996). *Designing standards-based districts, schools, and classrooms.* Alexandria, VA: Association for Supervision and Curriculum Development.

Marzano, R.J. & Kendall, J.S. (1999, January). *Awash in a sea of standards.* Aurora, CO: Mid-continent Regional Educational Laboratory.

Mathematics grade-level gap. (2000, February). *DataWorks Assessment Newsletter, 2,* (1), p. 1.

Milwaukee Public Schools. (2000). *1998-99 Accountability Report.* Milwaukee, WI: Author.

Mitchell, R. (1992). *Testing for learning: How new approaches to evaluation can improve American schools.* New York, NY: The Free Press.

Noyce, P., Perda, D., and Traver, R. (2000, February). Creating data-driven schools. *Educational Leadership*, *57* (5), 52 – 56.

Perkins, D. (1995). *Outsmarting IQ: The emerging science of learnable intelligence.* New York: The Free Press.

Peters, T. & Waterman, R.H. (1988). *In search of excellence: Lessons from America's best-run companies.* New York, NY: Warner Books.

Popham, J. (1999). *Testing! Testing!: What every parent should know about school tests.* Needham Heights, MA: Allyn and Bacon.

Public Agenda (2000, Spring). A sense of calling: Who teaches and why. [On line]. Available: www.publicagenda.org.

Reeves, D.B. (2002). *Making standards work: How to implement standards-based assessments in the classroom, school, and district.* Englewood, CO: Lead + Learn Press.

Reeves, D.B. (2004). *Accountability in action: A blueprint for learning organizations*. (2nd ed.). Englewood, CO: Lead + Learn Press.

Reeves, D.B. (2000, December). Essential Transformations for the Secondary School. *NASSP Bulletin*, *84* (620).

Rogers, S., Ludington, J., & Graham, S. (1998). *Motivation and learning: a teacher's guide to building excitement for learning and igniting the drive for quality*. Evergreen, CO: Peak Learning Systems.

Rothman, R. (1995). *Measuring up: Standards, assessment, and school reform.* San Francisco, CA: Jossey-Bass.

Schmoker, M.J. (1999) *Results: The key to continuous school improvement*. (2nd ed.). Alexandria, VA: Association for Supervision and Curriculum Development.

Viadero, D. (1999, May 5). Research notes: Sports and school success. *Education Week*, *18* (34), 29.

Wheatley, M.J. (1999) *Leadership and the new science revised: Discovering order in a chaotic world.* San Francisco: Berrett-Koehler Publishers.

Wiggins, G. (1998). *Educative assessment.* San Francisco, CA: Jossey-Bass.

Wiggins, G., & McTighe, J. (1998). *Understanding by design.* Alexandria, VA: Association for Supervision and Curriculum Development.

Wong, H.K. (1999, April). *There is only one way to improve student achievement.* Paper prepared for the National Conference on Urban Education, Jersey City, NJ.

Appendices

Appendix A

Standards Implementation Checklists

Classroom Checklist

Professional Practice	Exemplary	Proficient	Progressing	Remarks
1. Standards are highly visible in the classroom. The standards are expressed in language that the students understand.				
2. Examples of "exemplary" student work are displayed throughout the classroom.				
3. Students can spontaneously explain what "proficient" work means for each assignment.				
4. For every assignment, project, or test, the teacher publishes in advance the explicit expectations for "proficient" work.				
5. Student evaluation is always done according to the standards and scoring guide criteria and *never* done based on a "curve."				
6. The teacher can explain to any parent or other stakeholder the specific expectations of students for the year.				
7. The teacher has the flexibility to vary the length and quantity of curriculum content on a day to day basis in order to insure that students receive more time on the most critical subjects.				
8. Commonly used standards, such as those for written expression, are reinforced in every subject area. In other words, "spelling always counts" —even in math, science, music and every other discipline.				

Classroom Checklist (continued)

Professional Practice	Exemplary	Proficient	Progressing	Remarks
9. The teacher has created at least one standards-based performance assessment in the past month.				
10. The teacher exchanges student work (accompanied by a scoring guide) with a colleague for review and evaluation at least once every two weeks.				
11. The teacher provides feedback to students and parents about the quality of student work compared to the standards—not compared to other students.				
12. The teacher helps to build a community consensus in the classroom and with other stakeholders for standards and high expectations of all students.				
13. The teacher uses a variety of assessment tecyhniques, including (but not limited to) extended written responses, in all disciplines.				
Other professional practices appropriate for your classroom:				

School Checklist

Professional Practice	Exemplary	Proficient	Progressing	Remarks
1. A Standards/Class matrix (standards across the top, classes on the left side) is in a prominent location. Each box indicates the correspondence between a class and the standards. Faculty members and school leaders discuss areas of overlap and standards that are not sufficiently addressed.				
2. Standards are visible throughout the school and in every classroom.				
3. The school leaders use every opportunity for parent communication to build a community consensus for rigorous standards and high expectations for all students.				
4. Information about rigorous standards and high expectations is a specific part of the agenda of every faculty meeting, site council meeting, and parent organization meeting.				
5. The principal personally evaluates some student projects or papers compared to a school-wide or district-wide standard.				
6. The principal personally evaluates selected student portfolios compared to a school-wide or district-wide standard.				
7. Examples of "exemplary" student papers are highly visible.				
8. Job interview committees explicitly inquire about the views of a candidate about standards, performance assessment, and instructional methods for helping all students achieve high standards.				

School Checklist (continued)

Professional Practice	Exemplary	Proficient	Progressing	Remarks
9. A "jump-start" program is available to enhance the professional education of new teachers who do not have an extensive background in standards and assessment techniques.				
10. Every discretionary dollar spent on staff development and instructional support is specifically linked to student achievement, high standards, and improved assessment.				
11. Faculty meetings are used for structured collaboration with a focus on student work - not for the making of announcements.				
12. The principal personally reviews the assessment and instructional techniques used by teachers as part of the personnel review and evaluation process. The principal specifically considers the link between teacher assessments and standards.				
Other professional practices appropriate for your school:				

District/State/System Checklist

Professional Practice	Exemplary	Proficient	Progressing	Remarks
1. The system has an accountability plan that is linked to student achievement of standards - not to the competition of schools with one another.				
2. The system has a program for monitoring the "antecedents of excellence" - that is, the strategies that schools use to achieve high standards. The monitoring system does not depend on test scores alone.				
3. The system explicitly authorizes teachers to modify the curriculum guides in quantity and emphasis so that student needs for core academic requirements in math, science, language arts and social studies are met.				
4. The system publishes the "best practices in standards-based assessment" on an annual basis, recognizing the creative efforts of teachers and administrators.				
5. The system has established an assessment task force to monitor the implementation of effective and fair assessments, and to distribute models of educational assessments for use throughout the year.				
6. The system provides timely feedback on district-level assessments so that all assessments can be used to inform instruction during the current school year. Assessments that are not used for the purpose of informing instruction and improving student achievement are not used.				

District/State/System Checklist (continued)

Professional Practice	Exemplary	Proficient	Progressing	Remarks
7. The system reports to the public a comprehensive set of student achievement results throughout the year.				
8. The system uses multiple methods of assessments for system-wide assessments. It never relies on a single indicator or single assessment method to represent student achievement.				
9. There is a clearly identified senior leader at the system level who is responsible for standards, assessment, and accountability, and who communicates this information clearly to all stakeholders.				
10. Commitment to standards is a criteria in all hiring decisions at all levels.				
11. The system monitors the investment of resources - including staff development, technology, and capital expenditures - for a consistent and clear link to student achievement of standards. System leaders can provide explicit examples of changes in resource allocation decisions that reflect this commitment.				
12. Evaluations of schools and of building leaders are based on student achievement - not based on competition or any other norm-referenced system.				

District/State/System Checklist (continued)

Professional Practice	Exemplary	Proficient	Progressing	Remarks
13. The system does not take into account ethnicity and socio-economic level in determining its expectations of student performance. These variables, along with linguistic background, learning disabilities, and other factors, are included in resource allocation decisions and the development of instructional and assessment strategies.				
14. The system allocates resources based on student needs and a commitment to the opportunity for all students to achieve standards. Resources are not allocated merely on the basis of student population - the objective is equity of opportunity, not equality of distribution.				
Other professional practices appropriate for your system:				

Appendix B

Power Standards for the Middle Grades

The Need for "Power Standards"

Every school district in the nation has some form of local or state academic content standards. These standards describe what students are expected to know and be able to do. The standards do not, however, give the classroom teacher and school leader clarity about which standards are the most important for future success. Because of the limitations of time and the extraordinary variety in learning backgrounds of middle school students, teachers and leaders need focus and clarity in order to prepare their students for success in high school. Power Standards help to provide that focus and clarity.

Grades Are Not Enough: Students Must Be Proficient

In a recent study of middle schools conducted by The Leadership and Learning Center, the difference in average grade-point average for those students attending high-achieving middle schools was one-tenth of one point higher than the GPA for those students attending very low-achieving middle schools. In other words, grades typically do not tell students if they are adequately prepared for high school. By contrast, the requirement that students demonstrate proficiency at a few Power Standards is a clear and consistent mandate for high expectations and adequate preparation.

Making Time the Variable

In a traditional middle school setting, students in a 7th grade classroom may have reading levels ranging from 3rd grade to 12th grade. The assumption that all of these students will become proficient in the same amount of time with the same amount of teaching is absurd. In the typical uniform curriculum and standard schedule, these students will leave middle school with the same widely varying abilities with which they entered. Unfortunately, this means that many of these students will enter high school woefully unprepared for the challenges they will face. The clear and simple truth is this: some students need more time to become proficient. Placing all students in the same schedule and expecting uniform results is prescription for failure. Some students need more time for literacy and math. Denying them this extra time is as harmful as denying unvaccinated students the appropriate medical treatment because "they should have had the vaccinations before they got to middle school."

What About the Other Parts of the Curriculum?

The Power Standards are definitely not exhaustive. They represent the "core of the core" – the essential knowledge and skills students must have to enter high school. If they do not have these skills at the beginning of 8th grade, teachers and school leaders should insure that the students receive the schedule, curriculum, coaching, and intervention necessary to insure proficiency in these Power Standards.

What Middle School Students Need to Enter High School With Confidence and Success

Writing, Reading, and Social Studies

Students will use Standard English, including proper grammar, spelling, and punctuation, to complete the following independently evaluated essays. Teachers will evaluate the essays using the same district-wide writing rubric that is routinely used in the classroom for all writing assignments.

- ***Narrative***: Given a new short story of approximately 1,500 words, students will write a five-paragraph essay describing the setting, characters, and plot.
- ***Analytical***: Write a five-paragraph essay comparing the points of view expressed in two authentic historical documents.
- ***Persuasive***: Write a letter to the editor of a local newspaper expressing a point of view on a topic of interest. Include evidence to support your point of view.

Mathematics and Science

- Perform number operations (addition, subtraction, multiplication and division) from ten-thousandths to millions with and without a calculator.
- Given a story problem presented in narrative form, draw a picture that describes the problem and write word and number sentences that describe the steps to the solution.
- Draw an accurate two-dimensional scale drawing of a real world object. Include a demonstration of an understanding of the properties of rectangles and triangles, complete linear and area measurements, and accurate use of scale.

- Given a scientific question, generate a hypothesis, design an experiment, conduct measurements of at least two variables, place the data in a table, create an appropriate graph from the data in the table, and write a paragraph that correctly states the conclusions to be drawn from the experiment.

Teamwork, Organization and Service

Participate in a team in which each student shares responsibility for planning, organization, and execution of an original idea with value to fellow students and school community. Submit the project to evaluation by teachers and other adults.

Performance and Self-Confidence

Participate in one or more opportunities for personal excellence in music, art, drama, speech, athletics, or other individual endeavor that involves personal performance before an audience of adults and peers.

Developing Your Own "Power Standards"

In order to develop your own "power standards," it is essential to apply these three criteria to each unit, activity, curriculum element, standard, and test objective that might find its way into your classrooms:

1. ***Endurance*** – Will this provide students with knowledge and skills that will be of value beyond a single test date? For example, proficiency reading will endure throughout a student's academic career and professional life.
2. ***Leverage*** – Will this provide knowledge and skills that will be of value in multiple disciplines? For example, proficiency in creating graphs, tables, and charts and the ability to draw accurate inferences from them will help students in math, science, social studies, and language arts. The ability to write an analytical and persuasive essay will similarly help students in every academic discipline.
3. ***Readiness for the next level of learning*** – Will this provide students with essential knowledge and skills that are necessary for success in the next grade or the next level of instruction? For example, 4th grade teachers are unanimous that reading comprehension and math facts are essential for 3rd graders who wish to enter the 4th grade confidently and pursue 4th grade studies successfully. Those same 4th grade teachers are not unanimous that the ability to assemble a leaf collection, identify dinosaurs, or know the state capitals are required knowledge for entry into 4th grade.

Considering these three criteria, identify the "power standards" for students who will enter your class. That is, if you are a 6th grade teacher, identify the essential knowledge and skills for 5th grade students. If you are a 3rd grade teacher, identify the essential knowledge and skills for 2nd grade students, and so on.

My recommendations for "power standards" for students completing grade______:

"Power Standard"	Proficiency – Please describe specifically what students must know and be able to do	Remarks and explanatory comments
1.		
2.		
3.		
4.		
5.		
6.		
7.		

Appendix C

Sample Standards Achievement Report

Language Arts Standards	4 Exemplary Date	3 Proficient Date	2 Progressing* Date	1 Does Not Meet* Date
Write and speak for a variety of purposes and for diverse audiences. **Description of Evidence**				
Write and speak using conventional grammar, usage, sentence structure, punctuation, capitalization, and spelling. **Description of Evidence**				
Read and understand a variety of materials. **Description of Evidence**				
Apply thinking skills to reading, writing, speaking, listening, and viewing. **Description of Evidence**				

Sample Standards Achievement Report

Teacher Comments:

***Plan for Meeting Standards:**

Parent Comments:

Appendix D

Sample Standards-Based Report Card

RIVERSIDE UNIFIED SCHOOL DISTRICT
Elementary Report Card

Student s Name ______________________ **School** ______________________

School Year ______________________ **Teacher** ______________________

Grade ____________ **Date Enrolled** ______________________

SUBJECT GRADES	1st		2nd		3rd	
	Grade	Effort	Grade	Effort	Grade	Effort
Reading						
Writing						
Spelling						
Mathematics						
History/Social Science						
Science						
Penmanship						
Visual Arts						
Performing Arts						
Physical Education						

Attendance	1st	2nd	3rd
Absences			
Tardies			
Marked if absences/tardies negatively affect achievement			

GRADES 4-6

STANDARDS FOR GRADES 4-6
Proficiency level marked with an X

			1st Trimester				2nd Trimester				3rd Trimester			
			Below Basic	Basic	Proficient	Advanced	Below Basic	Basic	Proficient	Advanced	Below Basic	Basic	Proficient	Advanced
Language Arts Standards														
1	**Listening:**	Listens, comprehends, and analyzes												
2	**Speaking:**	Organizes and delivers oral communications												
3	**Reading:**	Analyzes words and develops vocabulary												
4	**Reading:**	Reads, comprehends, interprets, and evaluates												
5	**Reading:**	Analyzes and responds to literature												
6	**Writing:**	Conveys a clear, coherent message using correct mechanics												
7	**Writing Applications:**	Writes for various purposes and audiences												
Mathematics Strands (Only those strands currently being taught will be marked each grading period.)														
1	**Number Sense:**	Place value and computation												
2	**Algebra and Functions:**	Patterns and use of number sentences												
3	**Measurement and Geometry:**	Units of measure; description and comparison of shapes												
4	**Statistics, Data Analysis, and Probability:**	Understanding, use, and representation of data												
5	Mathematical Reasoning:	Organization and solution of problems												

Characteristics of Successful Students	1st	2nd	3rd
Uses time productively			
Completes classwork			
Completes and returns homework			
Respects the rights of others			
Follows class rules			
Follows school rules			

Marked if language arts instruction is in Spanish			
Marked if language arts grades reflect transition to English			

Marked if at risk of retention			
Marked if conference needed			
Next Year's Placement			

Special Program Participation if marked with an "X"	1st	2nd	3rd
Special Education			
Adapted Physical Education			
Speech and Language Services			
Resource Specialist Program			
Special Day Class			
Other:			
Gifted and Talented Education			
English Learner			
Structured English Immersion			
Bilingual Education			
Mainstream			
Title I			
Other:			

26-5565

RIVERSIDE UNIFIED SCHOOL DISTRICT

Elementary Report Card

Addendum for English Learners

Student s Name________________________ School ________________________

School Year ________________________ Teacher ________________________

ENGLISH LANGUAGE DEVELOPMENT Date Enr olled ________________________

SUBJECT GRADES	1st		2nd		3rd	
	Grade	Effort	Grade	Effort	Grade	Effort
English Language Development						

PHASE	1st	2nd	3rd
English Language Development			

STANDARDS FOR GRADES K-6

Proficiency level marked with an X

			1st Trimester				2nd Trimester				3rd Trimester			
			Below Basic	Basic	Proficient	Advanced	Below Basic	Basic	Proficient	Advanced	Below Basic	Basic	Proficient	Advanced
English Language Development for English Learners (Each standard may not be marked each grading period.)														
1	Listening:	Comprehension												
2	Speaking:	Recitations and oral presentations												
3-5	Reading:	Determines word meaning, comprehends, responds to literature												
6-7	Writing:	Clear, coherent, conveys message												
8	Links with Other Content Areas:	Participates in content instruction												
9	Personal and Safety Needs:	Expresses needs												
10	Beyond the Classr oom:	Interacts appropriately with others												

Standards Achievement Levels:

Below Basic: Lacking phase level knowledge and skills
Basic: Minimal phase level knowledge and skills
Pr oficient: Phase level knowledge and
Advanced: Ready to move to the next phase

Stages of English Language Development

Beginning Stage (Phase 1)
A student new to the English language is in this stage. In the initial months, the student has very little understanding but gradually begins to develop basic understanding of what is being communicated. He/she begins to produce one- or two-word responses based on familiar information presented to him/her.

Early-Intermediate (Phase 2)
Within one or two years of beginning to learn English, the student s understanding grows, especially in situations where the information is familiar. Students at this stage produce short phrases and simple sentences in English.

Intermediate (Phase 3)
At this phase the student speaks in more complex sentences, but still makes errors. Increased understanding makes it easy for the student to participate in everyday conversations. Usually, students reach this phase within two or three years of beginning to learn English.

Early Advanced (Phase 4)
A student at this phase is past the Intermediate Level (Phase 3) but still makes speaking and written errors in English. The student is able to participate in classroom academic discussions. Although the student makes errors in speaking and writing English, these do not interfere with communication. A student at Phase 4 may stay at this level if not given additional instruction. Additional instruction should develop speed of speaking and writing and should increase academic vocabulary.

Advanced (Phase 5)
The final phase is comprised of students who are ready to be fluent English speakers and writers. There are still some areas in English grammar, mechanics, spelling, and vocabulary that need to be improved. Once these are improved, the student will demonstrate native-like speaking and writing. The English language needs of the student in this phase should be determined on an individual basis.

26-5590

The Sample Standards-Based Report Card was reproduced with permission of the Riverside Unified School District, Riverside, California.

Appendix E

Sample Scoring Guides

Oral Presentation Student Scoring Guide: Elementary

4 Exemplary

- ❑ My presentation meets all the criteria under Proficient.
- ❑ I completed advanced work. For example, my presentation is not only informative, but also interesting to my audience. Other ways my presentation is extra great include: ______________________________

  ____

3 Proficient

- ❑ My presentation is logical and organized.
- ❑ It has a beginning, middle, and end.
- ❑ I spoke in complete thoughts, making sure to use correct grammar.
- ❑ I supported my ideas.
- ❑ I was aware of my volume, enunciation, tone, and the rate at which I spoke.
- ❑ My gestures were natural.
- ❑ I made eye contact with my audience.
- ❑ I had good posture.
- ❑ I answered questions from the audience.

2 Progressing

- ❑ My presentation has seven or eight of the Proficient criteria.
- ❑ I will practice to improve my presentation.

1 Not meeting the standard(s)

- ❑ My presentation has less than seven of the Proficient criteria.
- ❑ I will practice and try again.

Oral Presentation Teacher Scoring Guide: Elementary

4 Exemplary

- ❑ Criteria in the Proficient category have been met.
- ❑ **The response includes advanced work. For example, the presentation is not only informative, but also exceptionally engaging. Other examples of advanced work include:** ______________________________
____

3 Proficient

- ❑ The presentation is logical and organized.
- ❑ It has a beginning, middle, and end.
- ❑ The student spoke in complete thoughts, making sure to use correct grammar.
- ❑ The student supported his/her ideas.
- ❑ The student was aware of his/her volume, enunciation, tone, and the rate at which he/she spoke.
- ❑ The gestures were natural.
- ❑ The student made eye contact with the audience.
- ❑ The student had good posture.
- ❑ The student accurately answered questions from the audience.

2 Progressing

- ❑ The presentation met seven or eight of the Proficient criteria.
- ❑ More work is needed.

1 Not meeting the standard(s)

- ❑ The presentation met less than six of the Proficient criteria.
- ❑ The student will practice and try again.

Middle School Informative Writing

4 Exemplary

- ❑ Criteria in the Proficient category have been met. More advanced work is included. For example, the introduction grabs the reader's attention. Other examples include: ______________________________

3 Proficient

- ❑ Content
  - The scope of the topic is appropriate for the length of the paper.
  - Specific details are given in a way that keeps the reader's attention. General, trivial statements are avoided.
  - The sentences are original.
- ❑ Organization
  - Every detail supports the topic sentence of the paragraph.
  - Every detail is in proper order.
  - The introduction and conclusion are included.
- ❑ Language/Word choice
  - The words are grade-level appropriate.
  - Information is presented using metaphors, analogies, or any other device that personalizes the information.
- ❑ Sentence structure
  - Complete sentences are used.
  - A variety of sentences are used.
  - Sentences begin in different ways.
- ❑ Mechanics
  - There are no spelling, punctuation, capitalization, or grammatical errors in the final copy.
- ❑ The Writing Process
  - The writing process was followed as directed in class.

2 Progressing

- Ten to twelve of the Proficient criteria are met.
- The paper needs revision and editing to meet the Proficient criteria.

1 Not meeting the standard(s)

- Less than ten of the Proficient criteria are met.
- The informative writing piece should be rewritten.

Middle School Science

4 Exemplary

- Criteria in the Proficient category have been successfully completed. The response includes advanced work. For example, the student interviews experts about the disease, describes the details of how the disease overcomes the body's defenses or describes various alternative ways the disease might progress. Other examples include: ____________________

  ____

3 Proficient

- The student selects a disease or problem and performs research into its effects on the human body.
- Several sources are used and document.
- The report includes a description of how the disease affects cells and how it progresses in humans.
- All of the information is correct and clearly presented.

2 Progressing

- Three of the Proficient criteria are met.
- More work is needed.

1 Not meeting the standard(s)

- Less than three Proficient criteria are met.
- The task should be repeated.

Graphical Representation: High School

4 **Exemplary**

- ❑ Criteria in the Proficient category have been met.
- ❑ **The response includes advanced work. For example, the student decides on and draws an alternative form of graph to present the data. The usefulness of the graphical form of the information is evaluated and compared to other graph options. The written inferences are exceptionally detailed and additional predictions and conclusions are given. The mathematical foundations for the predictions are clearly explained. Other examples of more advanced work include:**

  ____

  ____

3 **Proficient**

- ❑ The student chooses the best form of graph for the data (line, bar, etc.).
- ❑ The graph is titled, clearly labeled, and the scales are appropriate.
- ❑ The graph accurately includes all of the data in the set. (For a line or bar chart, the independent variables are presented on the x-axis and the dependent variable is presented on the y-axis.)
- ❑ The student makes accurate and clearly written inferences about the data in the graphs. These include determining the types of relationships between the variables and interpreting his or her findings by answering specific questions about the data.
- ❑ There are no errors in spelling or grammar in any written work.

2 **Progressing**

- ❑ Four of the criteria for a Proficient score are met.
- ❑ More work is needed.

1 **Not meeting the standard(s)**

- ❑ Less than four of the criteria for a Proficient score are met.
- ❑ The task should be repeated.

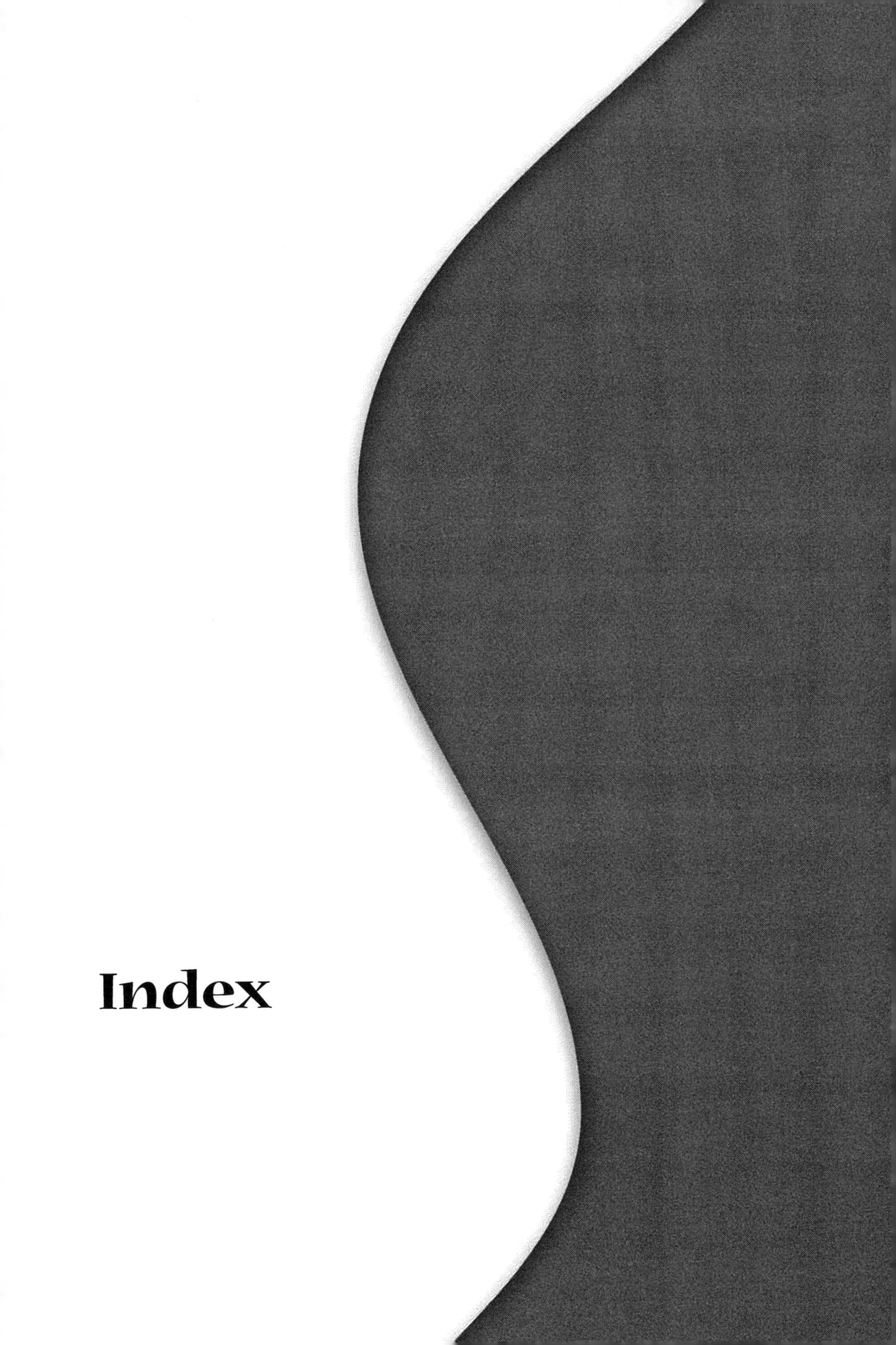

Index

A

B

C

L

M

N

P

R

S

T

U

V

W

Do you believe all students can succeed?

Can educators make a difference and produce results?

So much to do and so little time!

Since 1992, school districts and educational organizations seeking to improve student achievement have consulted with The Leadership and Learning Center. Educational leaders on five continents have collaboratively created customized solutions based on research and results. If you would like to know more about the services of The Leadership and Learning Center, to learn about success stories in every type of educational setting, to find out about the latest research, or to arrange a presentation by a Center consultant, please visit the Web site at at www.LeadandLearn.com or contact:

The Leadership and Learning Center
317 Inverness Way South, Suite 150
Englewood, Colorado 80112
+1.866.399.6019
Fax 303.504.9417